The Natural World *of* Winnie-the-Pooh

The Natural World of Winnie-the-Pooh

A walk through the forest that inspired the Hundred Acre Wood

By Kathryn Aalto

Timber Press
Portland, Oregon

Page 2: From *"In Which* Christopher Robin and Pooh Come to an Enchanted Place, and We Leave Them There" (*The House at Pooh Corner*)

Page 3: From *"In Which* a House Is Built at Pooh Corner for Eeyore" (*The House at Pooh Corner*)

Page 5: From *"In Which* Pooh and Piglet Go Hunting and Nearly Catch a Woozle" (*Winnie-the-Pooh*)

Page 6: From *"In Which* Piglet Does a Very Good Thing" (*The House at Pooh Corner*)

Pages 8–9: "The Hundred Acre Wood" (*Winnie-the-Pooh*)

Permissions and credits begin on page 295.

Thanks are offered to those who granted permission for use of materials but who are not named individually. While every reasonable effort has been made to contact copyright holders and secure permission for all materials reproduced in this work, we offer apologies for any instances in which this was not possible and for any inadvertent omissions.

The Haseltine Building
133 S.W. Second Avenue, Suite 450
Portland, Oregon 97204-3527
timberpress.com

Printed in China

Text, jacket, and binding design by Kristi Pfeffer

Library of Congress Cataloging-in-Publication Data

Aalto, Kathryn, author.
    The natural world of Winnie-the-Pooh: a walk through the forest that inspired the Hundred Acre Wood/Kathryn Aalto.—First edition.
        pages cm
    Includes bibliographical references and index.
    ISBN 978-1-60469-599-1
    1. Ashdown Forest (England) 2. Forests and forestry—England. 3. Winnie-the-Pooh (Fictitious character) 4. Milne, A. A. (Alan Alexander), 1882-1956—Homes and haunts. 5. Shepard, Ernest H. (Ernest Howard), 1879-1976—Homes and haunts. I. Title. II. Title: Exploring the real landscapes of the Hundred Acre Wood.
    DA670.A73A25 2015
    578.09422'5—dc23   2015009691

A catalog record for this book is also available from the British Library.

To the walkers
of the world
who know the beauty
is in the journey

CONTENTS

AND MR SHEPARD HELPD

Introduction

Reading A. A. Milne's stories for children is like tasting my grandmother's lemon meringue pie: the crust, tangy curd, and pile of meringue transport me to frothy, faraway days. In California summers, my large family gathered together in the dappled light of my grandparents' garden, and there were always lemon meringue pies. Those were carefree and fleeting times, when the most important thing I had to consider was which tree to climb and what direction to wander. The pie and these books are bound in nostalgia for bygone days.

Like you, I was read stories from *Winnie-the-Pooh* and *The House at Pooh Corner* at bedtime. Decades later, I have read the same stories to my children. The two teenagers cannot hide the twinkles in their eyes. Their younger brother rolls on the floor, clutching his sides with mirth and jollity. Their expressions reveal a tenderness for the adventures of the characters who inhabit the Hundred Acre Wood, a fictional landscape that is based on a real place in England. They still laugh zestfully at Milne's clever word-play, dry humor, and silly plot twists. They adore E. H. Shepard's sensitive illustrations, asking me to hold up the heavy red book just a little longer as Piglet tries to be brave or Pooh tries taming a slippery message-in-a-bottle.

A. A. Milne's prose is joyful, E. H. Shepard's drawings exquisite. Their collaboration created a classic, one of the most beloved and cherished children's books of all time. There is so much charm to Milne's writing in the way he captured a tender and free time of childhood, and created characters from an economy of words.

Winnie-the-Pooh is loyal and compassionate, playfully composing impromptu poetry and hums, and visiting friends for a smackerel of something. Like a four-, five-, or six-year-old, he is also a magical thinker: "If I plant a honeycomb outside my house, then it will grow up into a beehive." This and other admirable traits have inspired a plethora of books on philosophy, psychology, and literary criticism, including *The Tao of Pooh*, *Pooh and the Philosophers*, *Pooh and the Psychologists*, and *Postmodern Pooh*.

We know the bear's other friends as well. His best friend, Piglet, is nervous and timid, just a little fellow who often overcomes his fears at Pooh's side. And then there is Rabbit, who personifies the person of action; he is the best speller among the animals of the Hundred Acre Wood and he likes to organize, take charge and write bureaucratic Rissolutions. Out of earshot, Rabbit has said, "Owl, you and I have brains. The others have fluff. If there is any thinking to be done in this Forest—and when I say thinking I mean thinking—you and I must do it." Of course, we readers know Owl cannot even spell his own name (note "Wol") and especially not "Happy Birthday." Still, he is regarded as the wisest of the animals of the Hundred Acre Wood because he can use long words and is—well, long-winded. Dear Kanga is maternal and loving, while her little one, Roo, is always eager to try new things and test mother's boundaries. ("I can swim," says Roo. "I fell into the river, and I swimmed.") If a person is feeling "a bit like Eeyore," everybody knows this means gloom and pessimism have settled in. Eeyore's counterpart is the effervescent Tigger. Introduced in the second book, *The House at Pooh Corner*, Tigger is the most exuberant of the forest animals, but he has issues with self-restraint and controlling his bounce. ("I didn't bounce, I coughed," he says when accused of hooshing Eeyore into the stream during a novel game of Poohsticks.)

Last but not least, there is Christopher Robin. He is the benevolent and gentle child leader of the forest, a friend to all, and one of the most famous characters in children's literature. He was also A. A. Milne's real son, and his menagerie of stuffed animals provided the inspiration for these tales in an equally real place called Ashdown Forest, a landscape of sweeping heathland and atmospheric woodlands thirty miles south of London. The forest is a man-made landscape distinctive for large and rare heathland punctuated by gorse and bracken. A plant native to western Europe and Africa, gorse is a thorny shrub, closely related to broom. Bracken is a large genus of coarse ferns, and heath is a family of woody, low-growing shrub. The forest was at the doorstep of Milne's home, Cotchford Farm, and the sweet tales of adventure and friendship were set here.

Time stands still in the fictional Hundred Acre Wood. In our childhood imaginations, the forest and woods where Winnie-the-Pooh and his friends wander might be a static place visited only when we were young. In the real setting of Ashdown Forest, of course, the living, breathing landscape has changed. Trees—so prevalent in the stories—grow and then die. Streams move and meander. Fires clear plants. Many places in the Hundred Acre

Wood, however, are much the same as they were in Milne's day—Poohsticks Bridge, the Enchanted Place, and Roo's Sandy Pit are just a few examples. We can visit those places.

For places no longer around, it is possible to read the landscape for its own stories. As a landscape historian and designer, I am trained to read the landscape like a text and to unfold narratives of the past through research, interviews, and photographs. I also know when it is time to chuck books for boots and go outside for a walk.

Few topics can possibly be as fun as researching the natural world of Winnie-the-Pooh. My interest in the topic began in 2007 when I moved from my farm in Washington State to Devon, England. Avid hiking in American wilderness led to serious walking in England. I fell in love with the vast and ancient network of public footpaths and bridleways on this island in the Atlantic. From cliffs in Cornwall to Scottish highlands, walking gave me, an expat, an intimate understanding of my new home across the pond. My family and I have walked paths winding over mountains in the Lake District, through flocks of sheep in Yorkshire, and along the rocky Cornwall coasts. The length of Britain fits into my home state of California, but legal rights to roam provide extraordinary access to the landscape, which I'd not experienced in the United States. Walking here also has a different feel. A circular ten-mile path, for example, can feel epic; it is not unusual to find a Bronze Age earth mound near a village with a Norse or Norman name where Roman ruins have been preserved.

A slow and intimate way to navigate a new place, walking adventures, as we also see with Christopher Robin, connect children with nature in wonderful ways. Each passing year as my children's accents changed from American to English, they also gained miles of new understanding about nature and culture. We recently walked the Coast-to-Coast Path, an iconic trail across the middle of England, from the Irish Sea to the North Sea. They picked up pebbles from the Irish Sea, stuffed them in their pockets, and threw them into the North Sea two weeks and two hundred miles later.

Once upon a time, a very long time ago now, about last Friday, Winnie-the-Pooh lived in a forest all by himself under the name of Sanders.

—From *"In Which* We Are Introduced to Winnie-the-Pooh and Some Bees, and the Stories Begin," *Winnie-the-Pooh*

Between the Lake District in the west and Yorkshire in the east, they found toads and bats, fell into bogs, and picked wildflower bouquets. They read maps and navigated over streams, through fields and up trails. They were troopers; I was the one with blisters.

At the same time, I was reading Ann Thwaite's superb biography *A. A. Milne: His Life*. Smitten by his unusual childhood in the natural world, I then read his autobiography, *It's Too Late Now*. I learned that *Winnie-the-Pooh* and *The House at Pooh Corner* were more than stories of a boy wandering the landscape with his imaginary chums, but were based in part on memories of Milne's own golden childhood. He gave the same freedom he had to his son, Christopher Robin, by moving from London to Ashdown Forest. Milne's books are favorites from my own childhood as well as my own children's, and I had to learn more. As I got to know him as a person, the stronger I felt his presence when visiting his home, Cotchford Farm, and walking in nearby Ashdown Forest. I wanted to write a book he would be proud of. This book is the result of passions for walking, landscapes, and literature—all things Milne loved and celebrates in his writing.

Since *Winnie-the-Pooh* and *The House at Pooh Corner* were published in 1926 and 1928, they have taken on greater meaning. We value the books for simple expressions of empathy, friendship, and kindness. The stories are classics as they express enduring values and open our hearts and minds to help us live well. But as I read about Milne and walked around England with my children, I saw how they also tell another story: the degree to which the nature of

childhood has changed in the ninety years since Milne wrote the stories. There is less freedom to let children roam and explore their natural and urban environments. There are more digital distractions for our children that keep them indoors and immobile, and heightened parental fears that do so as well.

Combined with E. H. Shepard's emotionally delicate illustrations, the stories feel like snapshots from a past we want to regain. At a time when there is so much talk about nature-deficit disorder, rising childhood obesity levels, reduced school recess, and overprotected childhoods, these stories and illustrations remind us of the joy in letting our children explore the natural world and the importance of imaginative play away from the eyes of parents. The real and imagined places of the Hundred Acre Wood are tender touchstones for the precious time of childhood. Milne's books remind us that aimless wandering and doing Nothing is actually a very big Something for little ones. A lot of walking and a lot of reading can instill an appreciation for landscapes and literature and a whole lot more. I hope you enjoy the journey through these pages.

Creation of a Classic

The
COLLABORATION
of A. A. MILNE
and
E. H. SHEPARD

The tales of Winnie-the-Pooh and his friends in the Hundred Acre Wood are classics not merely because of Milne's charming storytelling or Shepard's delicate illustrations. The books are products of a pitch-perfect interplay between artist and writer, their particular talents and sensitivities, and their own experiences of childhood.

The Life and Work of A. A. Milne

On a Sunday morning in East Sussex, A. A. Milne sketches a scene for a children's book, a creative departure for him and one that makes his publisher nervous. He looks out his wide study windows to the landscape: beyond his own writing desk, beyond Daphne's garden still bathed in shade, beyond the meadow and stream where treetops catch early morning light like fish in a net. Beyond is Ashdown Forest. In creating what would become one of the most memorable and beloved settings in children's literature, he mixes memories of his past and observations of the present. The Hundred Acre Wood will be influenced by the natural world outside this window, as well as the world he remembers from his own childhood: exploring native English meadows, hunting butterflies along the coast, bicycling across many shires, and climbing peaks in Wales with his brother.

A. A. Milne

Everybody's luck, good or ill, begins on the day on which he was born. I was lucky.

—A. A. Milne, *It's Too Late Now: The Autobiography of a Writer*

Near Mortimer Crescent, London

Alan Alexander Milne was born on 18 January 1882, to John Vine Milne and Sarah Maria Milne (née Heginbotham) at Henley House on Mortimer Road in Hampstead. Four miles northwest of Charing Cross in London, Hampstead is one of London's most iconic and well-preserved villages, a picturesque Georgian enclave of Victorian cottages, where there are pale pink cottages with blue doors, overflowing flower baskets hanging along narrow cobblestone streets, and a selection of tantalizing pubs with names like The Wells, The Flask, and The Garden Gate. Nearby Hampstead Heath, an ancient and beloved park of nearly eight hundred wooded, hilly, and rambling acres, overlooks London from a high sandy ridge and was a place, like Primrose Hill, where Alan and his brothers wandered and explored.

Though now populated by more millionaires than anywhere else in the United Kingdom, Hampstead has a rich literary and artistic heritage. Resident luminaries have included Keats, Shelley, Coleridge, Orwell, T. S. Eliot, H. G. Wells, Agatha Christie, Katherine

"Here at Gills Lap are commemorated A. A. Milne (1882–1956) and E. H. Shepard (1879–1976) who collaborated in the creation of 'Winnie-the-Pooh' and so captured the magic of Ashdown Forest and gave it to the world"

Mansfield, and Daphne du Maurier. Hampstead visitors would be advised to carry a guide to blue plaques which commemorate homes of notable painters, philosophers, writers, scientists, and politicians.

During Milne's childhood, Hampstead was less a posh enclave and more a London village. His parents were teachers, and Henley House was their well-regarded school for boys. As for his ancestry, there were Scottish stone masons and missionaries on his father's side and a swashbuckling admiral on his mother's. For an imaginative boy like Milne, it was far more captivating to identify with one of Nelson's captains at the Battle of Trafalgar—his grandmother's uncle, Admiral Sir William Hargood, who is immortalized in a stone monument at Bath Abbey—than, as Alan wrote, "a man who sat by the roadside, chipping stolidly at little heaps of granite." The past may have posited profound questions in young Alan's mind: What kind of life would he want? Would it be one chipping away at stone or, perhaps, one immortalized in stone?

The world knows Alan's fate would be the latter. There would be people and places which would guide him to an immortality very different from his uncle's. His legacy would not be born of military valor exhibited in an epic, bloody battle on the high seas. It would come from the gentle adventures of humble heroes in an enchanted forest.

John and Sarah had three sons—David Barrett Milne ("Barry"), Kenneth John, and Alan Alexander, each sixteen months apart in age. His father was very shy, humorous, and erudite. His mother was simple, wise, unemotional, and affectionate, he recalled in his autobiography, *It's Too Late Now*. "A mother's job is not to prevent wounds," he recalls, "but to bind up the wounded. She had the Victorian woman's complete faith in the rights of a father. It was he who was bringing us up. He conceded her the Little Lord Fauntleroy make-up and did his best to nullify its effect."

And so the boys, with their blue eyes and flaxen hair, submitted to the wishes of their mother by occasionally wearing velvet blazers and the loose trousers called knickerbockers. Their long hair, after enduring a night wrapped in curling papers, draped onto their lace collars.

The boys hated it. Their father tolerated it. Their mother loved it. Theirs was a very happy home indeed and their sons thrived.

At Henley House, there were two semi-detached villas. One side was for the family, the other for the school. The joint gardens were converted into a playground for the schoolboys, the majority of whom came from nearby residential districts Maida Vale and St. John's Wood and whose parents were involved in business and the arts.

In recounting his childhood, which, significantly, takes up half his autobiography, Alan humorously recalls his first contribution to the family Bible, the lore of which his father never tired of retelling. The incident was Milne's first great foray into letters at age two and three-quarters. Barry, who was close to five—and "the bad boy of the family," Milne recalled—was ready to be instructed in letters. It was felt that Ken, inclined to be naughty at three and three-quarters, ought to tag along and learn to read as well. Their nurse-governess hung large sight-reading sheets over a blackboard in their nursery, and, as Milne recalled of himself in the third person, "Baby Alan, good as gold, sucked his thumb in the corner and played with his toys." Words were put up on the board: cat, mat, bat. His father came into the room as reading lessons commenced, and, as Milne writes:

> Just as they were going to begin, Baby Alan, playing
> with a piece of string in his corner, said to anyone who
> was listening, "I can do it." Papa told him not to talk now,
> there was a darling, because they were busy. Alan tied
> another knot in his string, and said, "I can do it." Papa
> said, "S'sh, darling," picked up the pointer, pointed it to
> a word on the sheet and said, "What's that?" Barry and
> Ken frowned at it. It was on the tip of their tongues.
> Bat or mat?

His pudgy fingers toying with the string, Milne shouted out, "Cat!" It also spelled out other things to his parents: Baby Alan was a precocious child.

Was Milne truly "lucky," as he thinks? For being born capable to parents who gave him a happy childhood, perhaps. Milne was a bright boy, but we know that success never really happens alone. His parents, especially Papa, nurtured him in ways that would play a part in Alan's eventual literary legacy. Milne credits much to his father, whose intuitive teaching and gentle manner would, as we can see, help nurture one of the world's most beloved writers of children's literature. Father adored son, son adored father.

John and Sarah provided a warm, affectionate, and stimulating home life for their three boys. To feed their imaginations, the children were taken to museums and outings and read aloud books, including the tales of *Uncle Remus*, *Reynard the Fox*, *Aunt Judy's Magazine*, *The Quiver*, and *The Pilgrim's Progress*. And to nourish their spirits, they attended a Presbyterian church and enjoyed walking holidays.

Many children, you might say, are raised in settings such as this. A special something which set his father apart, even for the 1890s, was what John told his boys. He would say: "Keep out of doors as much as you can, and see all you can of nature: she has the most wonderful exhibition, always open and always free."

And Alan did. Encouraged by his father, Milne's love of the outdoors began in the gardens of his family's home in Hampstead village and soon extended outward. At a very young age, he was able to wander with his older brother Ken into semi-rural regions of London as well as the leafy wooded park of nearby Hampstead Heath. Located nearly four miles north of Trafalgar Square, the semi-wild park is an ancient and beloved part of London and a natural wonderland for children. This and other places would feed Milne's imagination.

The setting of the books that brought A. A. Milne his literary fame is based on real places—Ashdown Forest and the Five Hundred Acre Wood—both of which are near the village of Hartfield. The success of the books came not merely from stories about a boy and his animal chums romping through an imaginary Hundred Acre Wood. It came from the magical interplay between writer and artist, between words and images, and the touching perspectives on the fleeting nature of childhood. Milne's choice of E. H. Shepard, also a young father and then a cartoonist at *Punch* magazine, who in 1931 would illustrate the most popular edition of Kenneth Grahame's 1908 *The Wind in the Willows*, reflected his desire to warmly render memories of the interior and exterior landscapes of his own childhood, his son's childhood, and the one created from the wellsprings of his imagination.

Milne's stories and Shepard's drawings depict children as avid, independent explorers. This is how it can feel when we were very young. For each of us, the landscapes of our childhood come with a different set of building blocks that construct our perceptions of the world. Some of our most memorable encounters and sensations with the natural world are from our middle childhood—those halcyon years between ages six and twelve.

In recent years, there has been concern that the very nature of childhood has changed. People have begun questioning if there has already been a "last generation" to play outside. In *Last Child in the Woods*, author Richard Louv writes about the modern disconnection between children and nature and the importance of providing children some autonomy in the natural world. "Whatever shape nature takes, it offers each child an older, larger world separate from parents." He says, "Nature can frighten a child, too, and this fright serves a purpose, too. In nature, a child finds freedom, fantasy and privacy, a place distant from the adult world, a separate peace." Christopher Robin reflects the confident child in an imaginary natural world, and his adventures remind us of places we have been and could be losing. When we are young, tramping through forests also leaves footprints on paths well into our adulthoods. Throughout the writing of this book, for example, I heard laments from grandparents and parents about the diminishing range our children are now allowed to wander. Milne's childhood and his stories are touchstones of a paradise lost, of a bygone time that many—writers, psychologists, parents—believe is important in the development of a child. Movements are afoot for natural playgrounds and more time in nature to encourage dreaming, playing, and negotiating the world. With these rising concerns over the nature of childhood itself, Milne's books offer a reminder about the importance of freedom in nature.

Recollections of outdoor play as a child can be pleasant places to return when we're adults. Writer Edith Cobb studied the role of outdoor play on children's development during this magical time period. In her book *The Ecology of Imagination in Childhood*, she suggests that "adult memories of childhood, even when nostalgic and romantic, seldom suggest the need to be a child" again, but point to a deep desire to revisit childhood perceptions of the world.

For Milne, warm early memories of roaming the natural world with his brother Ken inspired him to create the setting for what would arguably become the greatest children's books of the twentieth century, touching generations, selling millions of copies, and being translated into dozens of languages. The books were richly inspired by his adventures with Ken and reflect themes of freedom, adventure, friendship, and cooperation. When Milne wrote about the Hundred Acre Wood, it was a way to revisit his own golden memories, as we shall soon find out.

And whether our favorite story involves the Expotition to the North Pole or facing fears about Woozles and Animals of Hostile Intent, each story is a small journey within a bigger one, an adventure in a forest with themes grounded in classic nature writing: the search for a lost pastoral haven, the depiction of a golden age with an element of play, discovery, and whimsy. This is much the way Winnie-the-Pooh and his friends go gallumping through their days: "Well, he was humming this hum to himself, and walking along gaily, wondering what everybody else was doing, and what it felt like being someone else, when suddenly he came to a sandy bank, and in the bank was a large hole. 'Aha!' said Pooh. (*Rum-tum-tiddle-um-tum.*)" And *Aha!* an adventure begins. The stories take readers on journeys, and many of us feel we know the Hundred Acre Wood as if it were our own back yard.

On holidays, Milne's father introduced them to a variety of English landscapes on walking tours where they had direct and indirect contact with animals and the elements. Walking with his father and Ken set the foundation for Milne's lifelong enjoyment of the landscape. He remembers that one of his favorite hymns was "All Things Bright and Beautiful." He liked it, "as far as one can like a hymn, for it had a scent of the country which distinguished it from its fellows." From an early report card, we also get a sense of Milne's enthusiasm for the natural sciences, if not his organizational skills. Milne dusts off a report card to share what was written about him as a student.

He leaves his books about; loses his pen; can't imagine what he did with this, and where he put that, but is convinced that it is somewhere. Clears his brain when asked a question by spurting out some nonsense, and then immediately gives a sensible reply. Can speak 556 words per minute, and writes more in three minutes than his instructor can read in thirty. Finds this a very interesting world, and would like to learn physiology, botany, geology, astronomy and everything else. Wishes to make collections of beetles, bones, butterflies, etc., and cannot determine whether Algebra is better than football or Euclid than a sponge-cake.

Who wrote this report? Milne's favorite teacher, of course. It was the school headmaster: his own father. If the secret of education is to respect the student's innate abilities, his father was brilliant, intuitive and sensitive, even ahead of Victorian times in outlook. His father's ability to read people also extended to his teaching staff. This included a young lecturer who caught the quiet headmaster's attention. "I am quite fond of your mind," John would say to him, appointing him the school's first Science Master. This new teacher would give the young Milne his first botany lessons, further cultivating his nascent interest in the natural world. It was the soon-to-be-famous literary giant H. G. Wells—a few short years before he became known as the father of science fiction with the 1897 novel *The War of the Worlds*.

Wells gave the boys a firm grasp of scientific principles and outdoor experiences. They took fieldtrips to nearby Primrose Hill, Hampstead Heath, the Natural History Museum, and the London Zoo. He taught the boys how to look closely at nature by teaching them all to illustrate lessons in anatomy and botany. He enriched lessons with an endless stream of tangible specimens, from frogs to wild botanical samples. He wrote to a brother in the country to have

H. G. Wells

boxes and boxes of wildflowers sent to the Henley House—dog daisies, dandelions, violets, and "in fact anything in that way, the meanest flowers that blow," Wells wrote in his 1934 *Experiment in Autobiography*. He wanted to bring the boys into direct contact with nature as much as possible.

Many years later, Wells recalled in his memoir how Milne's father was a "man who had my unstinted admiration and remained my friend throughout life," someone whose shy manner may have masked the way he "watched his boys closely and would slacken, intensify or change their work, with the skilled apprehension of their idiosyncrasies." Milne was indebted to Wells for the affection he felt toward his father, and they would be great lifelong friends.

Milne became an enthusiast—a lover of all things—because he was at his father's school and his father was an enthusiast, hiring equally ebullient educators. If his father loved mathematics, so did he. If he was no good at French, it was because his father wasn't his teacher, he said. Milne thought his father the best person, "by which I mean the most truly good, the most completely to be trusted, the

Hampstead Heath

most incapable of wrong. He was different from our conception of God only because he was funny, which one knew God was not." Milne wanted to please him, and thrived in the pursuit of it.

If children are flowers lovingly tended in a garden, Milne was an award-winning cultivar tended by a father who understood what he need to thrive. Everything Milne would be was inspired by his father's tenderness and example. However, it was his middle brother, Ken, with whom he had the strongest lifelong connection. Half-way in age between Barry and Alan, Ken could have chosen up or down for a playmate and companion. Fortunately for Milne, he chose his younger brother. Unfortunately for poor Ken, Milne was not only very bright but very competitive and always on the heels of, or preparing to soon overtake, Ken's own success. Whatever Ken did—from athletics to academics—his clever younger brother would soon meet and surpass him. Ken, Milne softly remembered, was never ruffled by this. For the rest of their lives together, they would be the best companions. The dedication in Milne's autobiography reads: "To the Memory of Kenneth John Milne, Who bore the worst of me and made the best of me."

When they were young, Alan and Ken were boyhood conspirators, adventurers, and collectors of butterflies, rocks, plants, and animals—dead or alive. "We were inseparable," Milne recalled.

"Sometimes, when fighting, so mixed up as to be indistinguishable. We never ceased to quarrel with each other, nor to feel the need of each other. Save for the fact that he hated cheese, we shared equally all belief, all knowledge, all ambition, all hope and all fear."

Their parents gave the boys a most wonderful gift: a childhood of aimless wandering and imaginative play. "Almost as babies," Milne recalled. "We were allowed to go [for] walks by ourselves anywhere, in London or in the country, but we kept to the rules, and [Papa] knew he could trust us." The two so loved their parents, and wanted to please both, that they fulfilled this contract. They could be trusted to be their own intrepid explorers in Victorian London and in the countryside where they took holidays. As a result, they had greater freedoms. Milne recalls:

> As a fact, we were given more freedom than most children. We had a habit of getting up early, and it seemed to be understood, at any rate by us, that, if we got up early, we could do what we liked, so long as we did not wake Papa and Mama. At one time we had a passion for hoops; not the slow wooden hoop, which is hit intermittently with a wooden stick until it falls lifeless into the gutter but the fiery iron hoop spurred by a hooked iron prong from which it can never escape. Even now I can recapture the authentic thrill of those early-morning raids on London, as we drove our hoops through little, blinded streets, clean and empty and unaware of us; never tiring as we should have tired with no magic circle of iron to lure us on; lured now into a remove world of tall, silent houses, pillared like temples, behind whose doors strange, unreal lives were lived; until at last we burst into the Bayswater Road, and wondered if anybody had ever run before from Kilburn to Bayswater Road, and what Papa would say when we told him.

In recalling his adventures with Ken, Milne gives us a fuller sense of the nature of a childhood that seems both commonplace yet very unusual. The summer Milne was seven, the Milne family rented a holiday house in Sevenoaks, a town twenty miles southeast of Charing Cross in western Kent, where a Gordon setter, without a collar and seemingly without a home, attached itself to the family. Dark chocolate in color with silky pendulous ears, the dog was immediately named Brownie. At the end of summer, they took him back to London and he became their own. Milne recalls Brownie was loyal and loving and, "with the possible exception of Papa, the most admirable character in the family." The boys adored Brownie's company on their adventures in the city and country.

Brownie appears in some of Milne's earliest verse for children. Brownie was a beloved friend throughout Milne's childhood, perhaps even a model for the animal companions that would wander the Hundred Acre Wood with the fictional Christopher Robin. Milne remembered one day in a field near Finchley Road when Brownie began frantically digging in the ground. Out dashed a mouse—not a common house mouse, but a live field mouse. Oh, but it got away! Rising to the importance of the moment, Brownie redoubled his efforts, Milne and Ken standing by in anticipation. Since it was a Sunday afternoon, the boys prayed and prayed. *Dig, dig, dig.* Dirt and clumps of grass flew in the air as the dog made a valiant effort to prove his hunting pluck. And suddenly, another mouse darted out. This time the boys were ready. Caught it! With cheers, they brought the furry brown creature home to live in a cage. They felt they were "real country boys who had caught a real country mouse with a real sporting dog. All secrets of the wild were ours." When the mouse died not long after, they buried it in their front garden among potted orchids, geraniums, and lobelias.

Play for the boys was beyond pavement and playgrounds. In the neighborhood of Finchley Road, now a major London thorough-fare bordering Hampstead, Milne spent many Sunday afternoons with Ken, on hands and knees, wielding a geological hammer. On

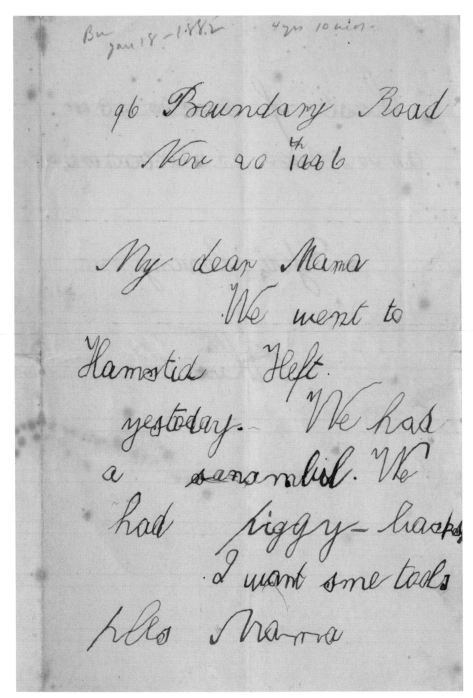

Letter from four-year-old Milne to his mother, describing his perambulation and piggy-back rides in Hampstead Heath.

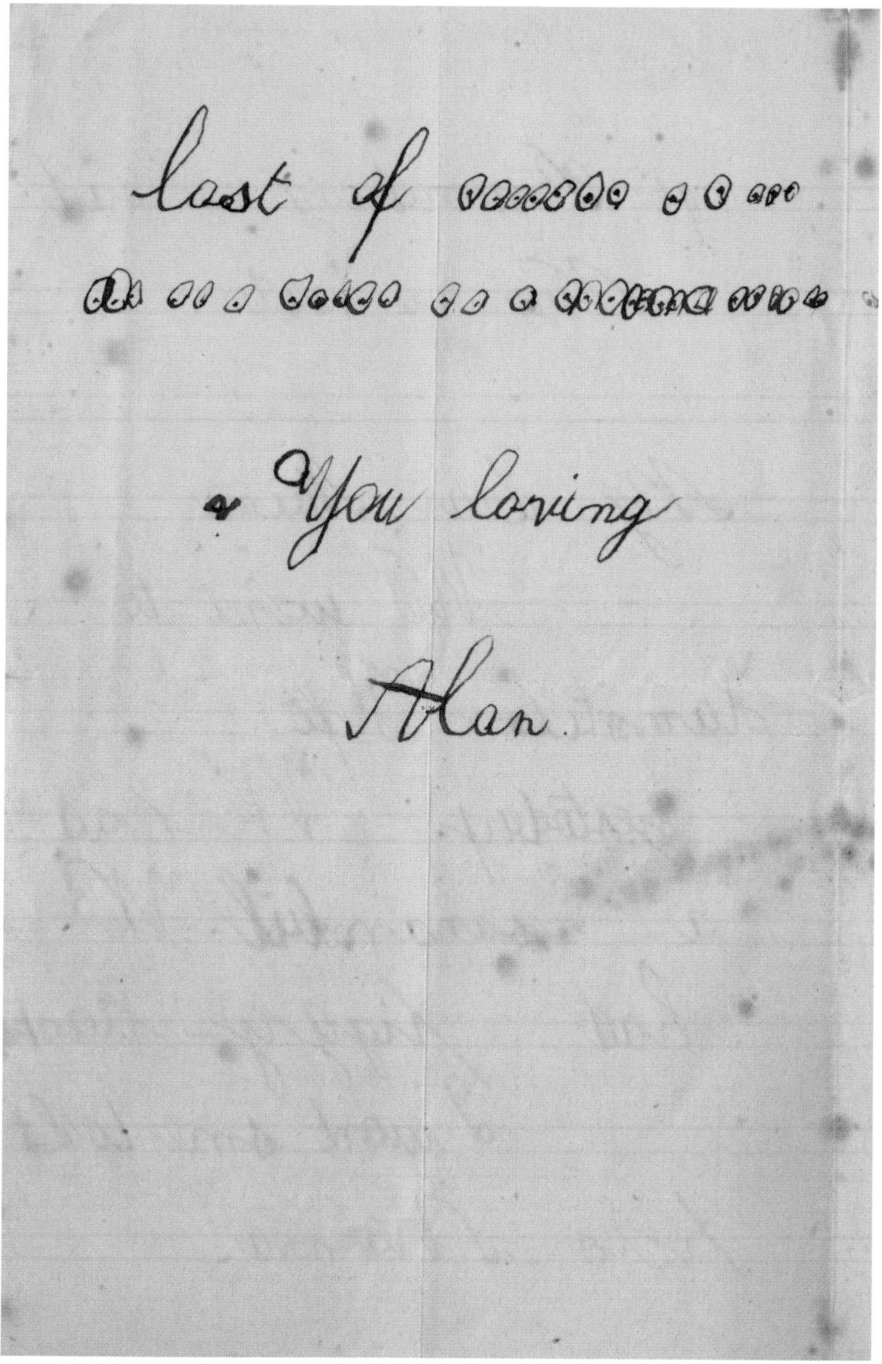

last of *uncertain text*

uncertain text

~ Your loving

Alan.

Hedgerow eggs like Milne collected: starlings, dunnocks, tits, wrens, finches, and sparrows

one Easter holiday, while attacking the white cliffs of Ramsgate with the hammers, they were inspired to start a collection of natural curiosities, including Iceland spar, Blue-John spar, crystals, ammonites, the fossilized remains of prehistoric animals, and, given the enthusiastic swinging of Milne's hammer, occasional chunks out of Ken's leg.

When Milne describes the walking tours of his childhood, the distances he covered are astonishing. He and Ken ambled over rolling English landscapes of native meadows, streams, and valleys. From an early age, he loved the outdoors. One such adventure, taken when he was just eight years old, was captured in an essay he wrote for school when he returned in the autumn.

Expeditions and explorations defined Ken's and Milne's boy-hoods. With long blond hair and other similar attributes, they looked like twins and even walked in time (in preparation for join-ing the Navy together, they dreamed). On another wild outing, per-haps in nearby Hampstead Heath or Primrose Hill, a large open grassy hill north of Regents Park, Milne fell out of a tree and lay breathless in the grass. Brownie bounded onto the scene in fine sporting style. He sniffed Alan once, then twice. But something else caught his attention. Their loyal hunting and adventure companion turned his snout toward a bumpy olive-colored thing in the grass. It was a toad, a magnificent toad! Whether it was dead or alive, Milne

My Three Days Walking Tour
by Alan Alexander Milne

WE WALKED TO EDENBRIDGE, six miles, and drank out of a pump—and while we were drinking a girl came to us and told us we were drinking river-water, so we went into a shop and bought some ginger-beer. After we had had a good drink we walked to Hever. When we got to Hever a distance of nine miles, we had a good dinner. While we were waiting for dinner we went over Hever Church and Castle, where Queen Anne Boleyn was born. We then had a lovely dinner of ham and eggs. Afterwards we went two miles across some fields and ate some lovely nuts, and then into a road which led to Chiding Stone. When we got there we bought some biscuits and some ginger-beer and we went on the Stone and ate them. Then we walked to Cowden. On the road we met a gentle-man who showed us the way (he him-self was going to the Isle of Wight). He left us at Cowden Station, which was a mile from the town. We then walked to Cowden, and here we hoped to have a rest. When we got there, we found there was no room at the inn! We then hurried away to the station a mile off, and took train to Tunbridge Wells. Here we found a lovely hotel called "Carlton Hotel"; we had a tre-mendous tea of ham and eggs, after a grand wash, and then went to bed. It was nineteen miles' walk that day altogether.

couldn't remember. Once little Alan caught his breath from the fall, he and Ken cut the creature open and removed its insides, gobsmacked at what little remained of the actual creature. They took it home, and, left unstuffed, what remained of the toad shriveled to dust in their drawer of rocks and minerals and other natural curiosities. Decades later in *It's Too Late Now*, Milne recalls the toad escapade and the complex naming of the amphibian's remains, and in doing so reveals his imagination and the touching bond he and Ken shared into adulthood:

> A secret so terrific, a deed so bloody, had to be formulated. The initial formula was Raw Toad (as you would have believed, if you had seen what we saw). Raw toad was R.T. which was "arte," and Latin for "by with or from art." Artus was a limb (or wasn't it?) and the first and last letters of limb were L.B. Lb. was pound; you talked about a "pig in the pound"; pig was P.G. and (Greek now, Ken had just begun Greek) πηγη was a fountain. So, ranging lightly over several languages, we had reached our mystic formula—"FN." Thumbs on the same hymn-book in Dr. Gibson's church, we would whisper, "FN" to each other and know that life was not all Sunday; side by side in the drawing room, hair newly brushed for visitors and in those damnable starched sailor suits, we would look "FN" at each other and be comforted.

Forty years later, these middle-aged men could look at each other, say "FN"—the cryptic name they gave the toad—and be transported to carefree field days with Brownie, to intrepid adventures and childhood freedoms.

One summer in the East Sussex coastal town of Seaford, the boys enjoyed a blissful time of hunting butterflies and collecting seashells. It was 1892, a peak year for clouded yellows, an immigrant butterfly originating in North Africa. The boys set out for

Clouded yellow

countless butterfly expeditions, sometimes together, sometimes alone. To indicate their catches from afar, Milne and Ken devised an elaborate method of communication: "Net at the trail in the right hand, nothing better than a small Tortoiseshell; in the left hand, Brimstone or Red Admiral; at the slope on the right shoulder, a Peacock or Painted Lady; on the left shoulder, Clouded Yellow; over the head, anything special."

The summers were always filled with adventures outside of London. Eventually the Milne family moved from Kilburn, London, to a seven-acre Elizabethan-era home on Street Court at Westgate-on-Sea. About that time, Milne felt his elysian childhood come to an end when Ken, at eleven years old, left home for boarding school at Westminster. Milne followed a year later with a full scholarship in mathematics. At age eleven, he was among the youngest students ever to receive the Queen's Scholarship. Though living at home together ended, his adventures with Ken continued in the summers

The Great Court at Milne's alma mater, Trinity College, Cambridge

on walking and cycling tours of landscapes throughout England and Wales.

During his boarding school days, Milne's mother, Sarah, would send the boys care packages which included bunches of flowers grown in her garden. They gave Milne "a nostalgia almost unbearable." The sight and scent of them "conveyed somehow all that I felt, but could not express, of Home and Beauty." When he returned home at the end of summer term, he was so cheered by the sight of them growing in her garden, writing, "Beneath our bedroom windows there was a dahlia bed, whose glory synchronized so steadily with the summer holidays that dahlias have made themselves a place for ever in my heart which their gaiety alone would not have given them."

Season after season, the colorful dahlias with sumptuous pom-poms and single flower heads grew and died back while the

Milne boys left home first for boarding school, then for university. Milne studied mathematics at Trinity College, later developing a more serious interest in writing verse and becoming editor of *Granta*, a distinguished periodical of student politics, badinage, and literature. After he graduated from Trinity in 1903, there were a handful of hungry years as he worked to establish himself as a freelance writer in London. H. G. Wells, who had stayed on friendly terms writing letters with Milne's father, was helpful to the young writer, advising him to always stay freelance. Wells encouraged him to join a society club and introduced him to William Archer, the prominent literary critic. A half dozen articles by A. A. Milne appeared in *Punch*, a venerable English weekly magazine of humor and satire. A shilling book was published, of which *The Sheffield Daily Independent* wrote, to Milne's dismay: "The only readable part of this book is the title." Terrified the publisher might want to print more, Milne bought back all rights to it. "Sometimes now I see it advertised in booksellers' catalogues," Milne dryly remarked in his autobiography. "It is marked, thank God, 'very rare.'"

In 1906, Milne was offered an assistant editor position at *Punch*. It paid £500 per year and was a turning point: no longer would he worry if he should have become a schoolmaster. He had new and different concerns, like meeting Friday deadlines for his weekly column. Though he was a prolific writer, it was not always easy to compose articles that were expected to have "a smile in every paragraph, and a laugh in every inch." In his autobiography, he said, "Ideas may drift into other writers' minds, but they do not drift my way. I have to go fetch them. I know no work manual or mental to equal the appalling heart-breaking anguish of fetching an idea from nowhere."

By 1910, he leapt from his assistant editor's desk to a seat at the *Punch* table of venerable writers and senior editors, many of whom had been contributing to the magazine longer than Milne had been alive. He had arrived. Like those before him, he was presented with a knife to carve his initials in the table, a quirky *Punch* tradition. "I

The Milnes' Mallord Street home

achieved a modest and monogrammatic A. A. M.," he wrote. During those years, Milne was prolific and wrote book reviews, critiqued plays, and submitted weekly articles for publication in *Punch*. These were the years when his writing, marked by a gift for humor and sharp, witty dialogue, brought him national and international acclaim.

Beyond his writing, we may wonder what Milne was like in person. In her superb biography *A. A. Milne: His Life*, author Ann Thwaite includes a 1913 description from the *Daily Citizen*, at which time Milne was thirty-one years old: "Like nearly all men of great humorous gifts, he is exceedingly sensitive and intuitive. A smile constantly plays about the corner of his mouth, and his eyes light up from time to time." When his son Christopher Robin recalled his father, it was a portrait of paradoxes: "shy, yet at the same time self-confident; modest, yet proud of what he had done; quiet, yet a good talker."

With sharp blue eyes, fine features, and a lean build from his love of sport, Milne cut a handsome figure as an up-and-coming Londoner, attending theater and dinners and meeting up with Ken. During these *Punch* years, he met the beautiful Dorothy de Sélincourt, a glamorous and witty young woman from a prominent family. Her father was Martin de Sélincourt, owner of the Swan & Edgar department store, a well-known place for generations of Londoners to meet. They carried a popular teddy bear called the Merrythought bear. However, the Milnes would buy their own famous bear, later named Winnie-the-Pooh by Christopher Robin, from Harrods. Daphne, as she was nicknamed, may not have shared Milne's passion for sport—golf and cricket—nor he her love of society—fashion and style—but together they enjoyed gardening, walking, conversation, and quiet places. She laughed at his jokes and she supported his writing. They were engaged in January of 1913 and married six months later. Christopher Robin debuted in 1920. Though it is little known, Daphne was an important part of the *Winnie-the-Pooh* books. When Christopher Robin was little, Daphne would play with him and his menagerie of stuffed animals, on the floor of their Mallord Street home in London. She was the first person to give voices and personalities to the characters who would call the Hundred Acre Wood home. She is indeed the "collaborator" whom Milne thanks at the end of *Winnie-the-Pooh*.

Through his writing at *Punch* and long before Winnie-the-Pooh toddled into his life, Milne rose in prominence to become one of England's foremost humorists. By the time he was thirty-five years old, his influence as a humorist was staggering. His ability to convey human nature in both a silly and sympathetic manner was the precise trait few could imitate. His columns at *Punch* became so popular that they were collected in bound volumes. In all these columns, plays, children's verse and prose, and later novels, Milne was able to capture human nature in a whimsical yet thoughtful manner. This sensitivity, humor, and wit can be seen in every chapter of *Winnie-the-Pooh* and *The House at Pooh Corner*. Recall, for example, when Pooh discovers that Eeyore has lost his tail and finds that Owl has been using it as a front door bell-pull. All the animals express great concern for each other when they lose their homes—Piglet's flooded home, Owl's blown-over home, and Eeyore's perceived lack of home. When Pooh consumes too much honey and condensed milk on a visit to Rabbit's house and gets wedged in the hole on his exit, Christopher Robin reads to him as he slims down over a week while Rabbit uses his legs as towel racks. Milne's expertise in droll dialogue and pacing of action are elements which he honed in writing for adults and transferred to his children's stories. These help make the stories so pleasurable. Silly misunderstandings and wordplay characterize interactions between characters of the Hundred Acre Wood, reflecting the confusion that young children experience as they are learning to grasp language. We see this in the story about the search for the North Pole.

> "Oh" Piglet," said Pooh excitedly, "we're going on an Expotition, all of us, with things to eat. To discover something."
>
> "To discover what?" said Piglet anxiously.
>
> "Oh! Just something."
>
> "Nothing fierce?"
>
> "Christopher Robin didn't say anything about fierce. He just said it had an 'x'."
>
> "It isn't their necks I mind," said Piglet earnestly. "It's their teeth. But if Christopher Robin is coming I don't mind anything."

In the years between 1903 and 1925 before Pooh brought him enduring international fame, Milne wrote eighteen plays and three novels. At one point, five of his plays were simultaneously running in London, New York, and Liverpool. Playwrights would complain that there was nothing but *Milne! Milne! Milne!* on stages. He was also an early screenwriter for the nascent British film industry. In 1920, he wrote four screenplays for Minerva Films, a company founded by the actor Leslie Howard, who had starred in one of Milne's most successful comedies, the 1919 *Mr. Pim Passes By*. A play still widely produced, it opened the 2014 season of Seattle's midsize Taproot Theatre which seats 150,000 people per year.

Whether it was writing the weekly humorous *Punch* columns or pivoting from plays to novels to poetry to essays, Milne had, according to his publisher Methuen, an exasperatingly independent streak. Most publishers are risk-averse. They want established authors to repeat past successes. But Milne wrote what he wanted and on his own terms. He left one genre when another caught his interest. Success begets success, and uncompromisingly he did not churn out what Methuen thought fashionable. Such levels of choice for a writer reveal the level of success he had reached. He could choose what he wanted to write. Fortunately, as he reflected in *It's Too Late Now*, "It has been my good fortune as a writer that what I have wanted to write has for the most part proved to be saleable." The downside to this, he noted wryly, is that "it has been my misfortune as a business man that, when it has proved to be extremely saleable, then I have not wanted to write it anymore."

It was natural during this prolific period as a playwright that he add a new genre to his writing repertoire: poetry and prose for children. Why? He always said that his writing was inspired from the life around him. And in 1920, there was indeed a new life—it was the year Christopher Robin was born. His father and mother called him Billy Moon—"Moon" being the result of Christopher Robin's first attempts at saying "Milne."

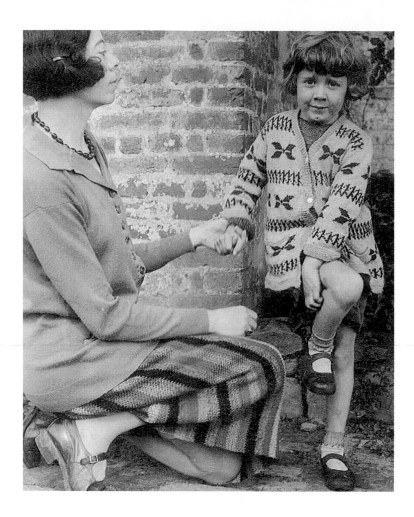

Daphne and
Christopher Robin,
about 1924

Milne's foray into children's poetry started when Daphne sent his first poem, "Vespers," to *Vanity Fair*. It was so positively received that "The Dormouse and the Doctor" soon followed. The illustrated proofs for this poem arrived in August 1923 when Milne, Daphne, and Billy Moon were on a holiday of unending rain in North Wales with friends. A *lot* of friends. And *friends* of friends. So many friends, in fact—the likes of which may have provided inspiration for Rabbit's Friends and Relations—that, feeling twitches of agoraphobia, the retiring Milne retreated to a summer house to write for eleven days, as he recalls in *It's Too Late Now*:

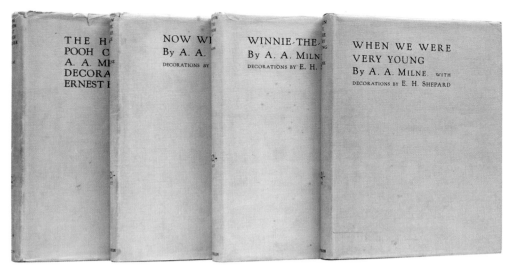

A set of Milne's
prose and poetry
for children

So there I was with an exercise-book and a pencil, and a fixed determination not to leave the heavenly solitude of that summer house until it stopped raining … and there in London were two people telling me what to write … and there on the other side of the lawn was a child with whom I had lived for three years … and here were my unforgettable memories of my own childhood … what was I writing? A child's book of verse, obviously. Not a whole book, of course; but to write a few would be fun— until I was tired of it. Besides, my pencil had an india-rubber at the back; just the thing for poetry.

The positive reception to these verses led to a succession of children's books in the mid-1920s. These included two collections of verse, *When We Were Very Young* (1924) and *Now We Are Six* (1927); a collection of twelve lesser-known children's fantasy stories called *A Gallery of Children* (1925); and two collections of stories we all know well: the eponymous *Winnie-the-Pooh* (1926) and *The House at Pooh Corner* (1928). By 1925, Milne was so famous that a splashy headline in the *Evening News* pronounced, "A Children's Story by A. A. Milne."

Methuen's advertisement for *Winnie-the-Pooh*

Milne continued to write successful plays during the 1920s—*To Have the Honour, Portrait of a Gentleman in Slippers, Success, Miss Marlow at Play, The Fourth Wall*—but what would bring him immortality? You and I know. The world knows. The gentle adventures of a teddy bear and his pals. The unanticipated, towering success of these stories took author, illustrator, and publisher by surprise. The books came at the height of his writing prowess and reflected the sum of his entire writing life: light verse honed in letters to Ken and for *Granta* magazine, humor polished at *Punch*, and brilliant dialogue sharpened as a playwright. "I wrote the children's books for my boy, Christopher Robin, commencing when he was four years old, in 1924, and ceasing when he reached his eighth birthday," he said in *The New York Times* during his one visit to the United States in 1931. As we know, the tales were inspired by his son's stuffed animals, each brought to life with distinctive personalities, and with the help of Daphne's imagination as well: Winnie-the-Pooh, Piglet, Rabbit, Eeyore, Kanga, Roo, Tigger, and Owl. Combined with E. H. Shepard's sensitive and masterful illustrations, *Winnie-the-Pooh* and *The House at Pooh Corner* have touched readers young and old for generations and are regarded as the most beloved books of children's literature in English.

Alan and Daphne Milne were Londoners through and through, but wanted to raise their son in the tranquility of the country, as they had known as children. In 1925, they bought Cotchford Farm in East Sussex, about an hour's drive south of London. The family visited the medieval-era farm on the edge of Ashdown Forest on weekends, a month at Easter, and two months in summer until they finally took full-time possession—or rather "Cotchford Farm took possession of us," several years later, as Christopher Robin wrote in his autobiography, *The Enchanted Places*.

For Daphne as much as Milne, nature was an elemental part of childhood. In contrast to Milne's more modest upbringing, the gardens of her childhood were the best money could buy. Daphne had been brought up both in London and in the Hampshire countryside at Brooklands on the Hamble, a Grade II-listed home—a British classification of a building of national importance and special interest—near Southampton. Historically, architecturally, and horticulturally, the pedigrees are faultless, as noted in the British weekly magazine *Country Life*. Christopher Robin remembered the colorful plants that grew there—and that served as the origin of his mother's deep love of gardening.

Milne in his garden at Cotchford Farm with Tattoo the tortoiseshell cat in his lap, about 1925

Daphne's childhood at Brooklands was different from Milne's on Mortimer Crescent in Hampstead, now a cluster of five-story apartment buildings. Both places reveal how Milne and Daphne came to love birds and bees, gardens, and landscapes—one a manicured version of nature, the other a wilder version. Indeed those involved in the design of Daphne's ancestral home read like a Who's Who of English home and garden history: John Nash, responsible for the layout of Regency London and Buckingham Palace, built Brooklands for Sir Thomas Williams in the 1800s. Sir Humphry Repton, regarded as the last great English landscape designer of the eighteenth century and successor to the even more famous garden designer Capability Brown, designed the twenty-nine-acre garden and summer house. Repton's landscapes include some of England's finest: from Tatton Park and Woburn Abbey to Longleat House and

HARTFIELD AND DISTRICT HORTICULTURAL SOCIETY
Affiliated to the Royal Horticultural Society

President—A. N. STUART, ESQ.

Vice-Presidents—
Lord De La Warr, Lady Evelyn Malcolm, Dr. Steel, J. R. Owen, Esq., A. A. Milne, Esq., Mrs. Owen, Mrs. Cooksey, Mrs. Stuart, Lord Castlestewart, H. Reeves, Esq., G. Schicht, Esq., Major Lonquet Higgins, Col. Paton, Lawrence Smith, Esq., F. Howe, Esq., Rev. J. C. C. Pepys

Hon. Life Vice-Presidents—
E. BALDWIN, ESQ.   G. ELLIOTT, ESQ.

SCHEDULE OF EXHIBITS—1947

THE EIGHTY-SIXTH ANNUAL

SUMMER SHOW

ON WEDNESDAY, JULY 30th

IN THE VILLAGE HALL and TOWN CROFT

•

THE SIXTEENTH ANNUAL

AUTUMN SHOW

On WEDNESDAY, NOVEMBER 5th

IN THE VILLAGE HALL

OFFICERS

Chairman of Committee	MR. M. CHESSON
Vice-Chairman of Committee	MR. J. TITHERIDGE
Hon. Secretary	MR. E. H. HERRINGTON
Hon. Treasurer	MRS. CHESSON

Milne served as vice-president of the Hartfield Horticultural Society.

Kensington Gardens. The list goes on. Sir Edwin Lutyens, known as the greatest British architect, designed an extension in 1916, and the pièce de résistance? His influential partner in the arts and crafts movement, Gertrude Jekyll, designed the expanse of manicured lawns, stone paths, and terraces, with borders full of her famously radiant flowers. What Christopher Robin most remembered about his mother's ancestral home was its annual awakening of the "colour and scent of azaleas" planted by Jekyll.

As Christopher Robin remembers it, his parents had an arrangement in the garden akin to ant and grasshopper: she was the gardener, he was the writer. She studied books by 1930s garden writer Marion Cran, first female radio announcer for the BBC, pored over seed catalogues, and, with memories of Brooklands to inspire her, designed terraces, rose gardens, and vibrant perennial borders. As for Milne, he was relegated a putting lawn for golf, a meadow for cricket, and a stream. A lifelong cricket fan, he was less gardener than sportsman in the garden. There was family talk of transforming that stream into a design feature with goldfish and water lilies. "But all it seemed able to grow were dense mats of brown weed," writes Christopher Robin. "And brown scum congealed on the surface." The only form of digging and weeding father and son did was when plunging nets and golf clubs into the pond to unearth various inhabitants, whether golf balls, snakes, or newts. As well as sport, the garden for Milne was a place to enjoy a book in the shade of a

Daphne's influence
in the garden layout
remains.

tree. Wilder landscapes outside the garden at Cotchford Farm were more of an interest for him, as he could walk and explore.

Milne's desire for tranquility and peace in the landscape also reflected personal beliefs: he was a pacifist, though he worked as a signaling officer in the bloody Battle of the Somme in World War I. He went into this war because he felt confident it was the war to end all wars. Documents thought to have been destroyed recently emerged, showing that Milne also worked as a propagandist for the secretive M17b between 1916 and 1918. He was enlisted to work as part of a small group of writers—some of the greatest writers of the age, including Cecil Street, Roger Pocock, and Patrick Mac-Gill—who used their skills to alter perceptions of front line realities and to boost morale back home. He was discharged in 1919.

A generation later, Cotchford Farm welcomed World War II evacuees. For several years, as biographer Thwaite noted, the rural setting of Cotchford Farm provided refuge for many children

Christopher Robin
and Winnie-the-Pooh

who enjoyed the fresh air, vegetables from Tasker's carefully tended gardens, and very likely some time with a great writer of children's literature.

Writing for children was a natural, though short-lived, episode in Milne's overall writing career. Again and again, his own golden childhood was a source of inspiration. Much of his autobiography is devoted to his middle childhood adventures. Christopher Robin said, "He wrote his autobiography because it gave him the opportunity to return to his boyhood—a boyhood from which all his inspiration sprang." Milne was an excellent listener and highly intuitive; his insights into all people, but especially children, were wonderfully keen. He wrote: "In as far as I understand their minds the understanding is based on the observation, casual enough and mostly unconscious, which I give to people generally: on memories of my own childhood and on the imagination which every writer must bring to memory and observation." He felt children possessed "an artless beauty, an innocent grace, an unstudied abandon of movement," and he endeavored to describe in an unsentimental fashion the natural charm and guileless innocence of a child.

In *Winnie-the-Pooh* and *The House at Pooh Corner*, Milne captured the fleeting time of life when, as children, our stuffed animals seem very real companions to us. He celebrated a most poignant part of our lives through these stories. For that inspiration, he could look no further than Christopher Robin for inspiration, since his quiet and imaginative son enjoyed his stuffed animals so much.

Then, eventually and sadly, childhood must come to an end for all of us. Milne knew this. We know this. We must grow up and leave behind our imaginary friends. But they never really leave us.

This happens in *The House at Pooh Corner* when Christopher Robin goes away. None of his forest friends know why he is leaving, nor do we readers. We are left to guess. In the final chapter, "*In Which* Christopher Robin and Pooh Come to an Enchanted Place, and We Leave Them There," Christopher Robin and Pooh walk through the long shadows of twilight. and Christopher Robin says, "What I like doing best is Nothing." As readers, we might wonder where this conversation is going. After wandering a bit, Christopher Robin lies down in a grassy area on Galleons Lap and ponders the changes coming in his life.

> Then, suddenly again, Christopher Robin, who was still looking at the world with his chin in his hands, called out "Pooh!"
> "Yes?" said Pooh.
> "When I'm—when—Pooh!"
> "Yes, Christopher Robin?"

"I'm not going to do Nothing any more."

"Never again?"

"Well, not so much. They don't let you."

Christopher Robin struggles to tell his friend that their time together is ending. To try to cheer himself, Christopher Robin says:

"Pooh, when I'm—you know—when I'm not doing Nothing, will you come up here sometimes?"

"Just me?"

"Yes, Pooh."

"Will you be here, too?"

"Yes, Pooh, I will be really. I promise I will be, Pooh."

"That's good," said Pooh.

"Pooh, promise you won't forget about me, ever. Not even when I'm a hundred."

When Christopher Robin asks his friend to visit the Enchanted Place, their adventures in the Hundred Acre Wood come to an end. It is a hushed moment of separation, one that we all experience when we step from one poignant landscape to another and a period of our lives is gone forever. The Christopher Robin who steps through the pages of the books is the child in all of us who must

The original stuffed animals on display in the Children's Center at 42nd Street inside the Stephen A. Schwarzman Building at the New York Public Library

Atop Kidd's Hill

leave behind Nothing for Something—perhaps that Something is the village kindergarten down the lane or a boarding school across country. Winnie-the-Pooh is the symbolic caretaker of those enchanting days of yore, the friend we have all played with during the day and cuddled at night. He is the tattered but treasured stuffed animal who waits for our return in an attic trunk or from the perch of a dusty shelf in our childhood bedrooms.

How does the story continue between Christopher Robin and Pooh bear? That is a narrative left to our imaginations. But we can return to that place, the Hundred Acre Wood, with its honey trees and sandy pits, rabbit holes and tree houses. It is not merely a fabled literary landscape that exists only in our minds. It is Ashdown Forest, a living landscape where Milne walked for decades and which inspired him to set these stories. You and I can visit it today. And if you and I can visit those enchanting places in more than our imaginations, is that time of our lives truly gone?

E. H. Shepard, 1932

The Life and Work of E. H. Shepard

With a few sensitive sweeps from his pen, Ernest Howard Shepard could capture nuanced feelings, complex gestures, and fine details in people and places. If the tales of Winnie-the-Pooh and his friends in the Hundred Acre Wood endure as classics, it is not merely because of Milne. Nor is it merely the illustrations. The books are a pitch-perfect collaboration and sensitive interplay between artist and writer, who had been contemporaries at *Punch*, and their own experiences of childhood. Their early lives are windows into how they interpreted the world later as author and artist. Their childhoods coalesced in these books, but for very different reasons: for Milne, it was born of great happiness in childhood; for Shepard, great sadness.

Shepard was born at St. John's Wood in North West London in 1879. He was the youngest of three children of Henry Dunkin Shepard, an architect with a love of the arts, and Harriet Jessie Lee, who encouraged her son's artistic talents. She was the daughter of William Lee, a prominent Victorian watercolorist whose large circle of notable artist friends gave their family home the quality of a salon, imbuing Harriet's childhood with an air of Bohemian artistry and instilling in her a serious interest in the arts. Henry and Harriet also had two other children, Ethel, who was born in 1876, and Cyril in 1878.

There was natural artistry in the family with a mother who showed him how to use paints and father talented with pen and pencil. Shepard's mother encouraged her children to use their inherited talents. She made sure he always had a notebook and pencil with him. Through time, he developed a photographic memory for drawing scenes, events, and gestures. He also modeled as a child for the notable Victorian painter and illustrator Sir Francis Dicksee, a family friend and later president of the Royal Academy, who was known for his historical and dramatic scenes as well as commercially successful, elegant portraits of stylish women.

Known throughout his life by family and friends as "Kipper," Shepard had a happy early childhood and Victorian-era family life in London. His childhood was filled with trips to art shows, violin lessons, shows on Drury Lane, and train rides to the country. He remembered Queen Victoria's Jubilee celebrations and drew them with vivid accuracy. There were summers on the seaside, homemade plays with family friends, and memorable family Christmas dinners. By his own recollection, it was a happy and idyllic childhood with loving parents who encouraged his talents and interests.

When he was eleven years old, however, the family narrative unfolded in an unexpected way. One day his mother, bedridden for months, bid the children a cheery goodbye for what they perhaps thought was a short trip to visit his aunts. Not much later, she died. The children knew she had been ill—they had been used to pushing her in a wheeled chair around parks and visiting with her while she lay in bed—but were unprepared for her death. They all loved and adored her and deeply missed her presence. Her death cast long shadows of grief through the family. Shepard said that he felt his childhood ended then. It would be years before anybody in the family regained a natural sense of happiness, he recalled in his autobiography, *Drawn from Life*.

To a child, the death of a parent can have long-lasting effects, and it was indeed so for Shepard and his siblings, but drawing continued to be an outlet of expression for him. Art was a way to stay tethered to his mother's artistic dreams for him. He was very talented, too. From his own suffering as a child, his empathy was deepened and his illustrated depictions of emotions—from uncertainty to jollity to melancholia—sharpened. Consider the way he portrays a contemplative or bewildered Pooh bear or a timid Piglet trying to be brave.

Simple yet sensitive gestures from "*In Which* Pooh and Piglet Go Hunting and Nearly Catch a Woozle" (*Winnie-the-Pooh*)

Shepard's drawing of Spanish conquistadores on the back of his Latin homework at age fourteen

Shepard's illustrations of naval battle scenes, soldiers with weapons drawn, and conquerors and conquistadors show his nascent talent through subjects that most interested him as a thirteen- and fourteen-year-old boy. His father loved theater and often brought his children to plays. Shepard brought his notebooks along, drawing all manner of scenes, including dances, military battles, and faraway places. He also captured the tableau of life around him, including small facets such as profiles of his four maiden aunts, as well as grander Victorian events such as the wedding procession of King George and Queen Mary through the streets of London.

Shepard attended St. Paul's School and entered the Academy School in 1898 on scholarship, later winning prizes and accolades for figure painting and drawing. It was in art school that he met Florence Eleanor Chaplin, a talented fellow student four years his senior and the granddaughter of Ebenezer Landsells, a founder of *Punch*, where Milne wrote. Shepard and Florence married, and their two children, Graham and Mary, were born in 1907 and 1909.

By 1906, he was an established illustrator working on editions of *Aesop's Fables* and *David Copperfield* and contributing occasional drawings to *Punch*. Like Milne, his career was interrupted by World War I, during which he served on the western and Italian fronts and commanded the 105 Siege Battery of the Royal Garrison Artillery. He was demobilized in 1919. In 1921 he embarked on a fifty-year career at *Punch*, providing political cartoons, jokes, and covers. Shepard and Milne knew each other's work through the magazine and became collaborators through *Punch* editor E. V. Lucas, himself a well-known and prolific writer. Lucas was also the celebrated head of Methuen and would become the original publishers of Milne's children's stories. Their partnership began when Shepard illustrated the 1924 collection of verses *When We Were Very Young*.

Milne's and Shepard's collaboration would produce one of the greatest celebrations of childhood. The atmospheric landscape, combined with Shepard's particularly sensitive drawings—of thoughtful Pooh, melancholy Eeyore, effervescent Tigger, timid Piglet, and all the other adorable creatures—are central to our warm regard for the stories. Milne knew this. He cultivated it. How the two worked together in the mid-1920s is a fascinating look into artists at the apex of their careers. Milne appreciated Shepard's role in the success of the books and—unheard of at the time—shared book royalties with him rather than pay a flat fee per illustration. This income would make Shepard a very comfortable artist indeed.

The emotions in the illustrations came from the inkwell of his heart and observations of real-life, but Milne also had a hand in matters. He expressed how he envisioned the stories and characters. Drawings evolved in conversations over tea and lunch, in letters between the two men, at the Milne home on Mallord Street in London, and, of course, on a visit to Hartfield. Unlike Picasso, who said, "I draw not what I see but what I think," Shepard drew from real life. In fact, his visual memory was so acute that he could re-create on paper events and people he remembered from years earlier. Knowing how Ashdown Forest inspired the stories and setting Milne created, Shepard visited and sketched Ashdown Forest in 1926, the two men walking to Poohsticks Bridge, Gills Lap, and elsewhere. The bee tree, Wol's tree, Galleons Lap, and the Enchanted Place were real places Shepard interpreted with a notebook, pen, and pencil in hand. He wanted to capture a tangible sense of place to set the adventures. He sketched pine trees and heathland and watched Christopher Robin making mud pies with Graham, Shepard's son, in the gardens at Cotchford Farm.

On a preliminary sketch of Ashdown Forest from 1926, Shepard wrote "Winnie the Pooh, Ashdown Forest 1926 (where it all happened) a sketch made on the spot when I visited it with A. A. Milne." We see low gorse shrubs and the open space of a landscape in the background. Another initial drawing, called "Tree for Wol's House," looks exactly like the view from the Five Hundred Acre Wood overlooking Wrens Warren.

At his small studio in Shamley Green near Guildford, Shepard worked in ink, pen, and black crayon on smooth art board or watercolor paper. He rarely rendered shadows in black and instead favored cross-hatching, fine line, or crayon. We see his loose pencil marks as he sizes up the character on the page, the development of the body, the tilt of the head, and tender facial expressions. We see Pooh's knees slightly buckle under the weight of a jar of honey he's carrying to the Heffalump Trap and his bewilderment as he stands on the branch of Wol's house trying to make sense of "PLEZ CNOKE IF A RNSR IS NOT REQID." There are poignant pencil drawings of rabbits, the nape of the neck of a tired Christopher Robin heading to bed, Winnie-the-Pooh fluffing his ears with brushes in the mirror, and the detail of the meadow where the North Pole is discovered.

Shepard's masterful illustrations were tenderly drawn from real life. He enhanced Milne's characters—their dialogue, manner, and adventures—to capture the charm Milne put in words. All the creatures were drawn from Christopher Robin's own stuffed animals except for one: Winnie-the-Pooh. This characterization was inspired by Growler, a teddy bear belonging to Shepard's son. Years later, Shepard recalled telling Milne, rather sheepishly, how Growler lost a fight with a dog in a Montreal garden. Perhaps they commiserated. Perhaps Milne felt relief. He, too, had a secret. Roo, he revealed, had met a similar fate in the jaws of a dog in a nearby orchard.

Milne and Shepard communicated in the old-fashioned manner of handwritten letters sent in stamped envelopes. Their correspondence shows a mutual appreciation for each other's vision and a warm and professional relationship. In cryptic, witty script, Milne wrote notes to accompany typed stories, complete or in parts, sent to Shepard for illustration. They began with "My dear Shepard" and other terms of endearment like "My dear Tubby." Some stories would be accompanied by longer letters detailing specific ideas he had in mind for staging an illustration, expressing an action, or portraying a character.

In 1925, Milne wrote a letter about the new map of the Hundred Acre Wood Shepard had drawn. It had everything in its right place, Milne said, but could Shepard please place each character outside his or her house? He also encourages Shepard to "put in as much as you like and show other bits of wood here and there." In another letter, Milne says he prefers having the Heffalump's head tilted upward for full dramatic effect. Could Shepard also create a diagonal table across two pages that would look like a picture of the friends of the forest having a party? Would Shepard please re-draw Christopher Robin, as he looks closer to nine years old and six is the ideal?

After *Winnie-the-Pooh* had been printed, Milne ends a letter by writing, "May I say how much we all love your pictures. You have really made a delightful book of it, and we ought to have an enormous sale." Milne admired the way Shepard sympathized with feelings Milne sought to convey in his writing. He felt so strongly for his illustrator's work that he inscribed Shepard's copy of *Winnie-the-Pooh*:

When I am gone,

Let Shepard decorate my tomb,

And put (if there is room)

Two pictures on the stone:

Piglet from page a hundred and eleven,

And Pooh and Piglet walking (157)...

And Peter, thinking that they are my own,

Will welcome me to Heaven.

    —A. A. MILNE

One of Milne's favorite drawings by Shepard, from *"In Which* Christopher Robin
Leads an Expotition to the North Pole" (*Winnie-the-Pooh*)

Nobody had any idea of potential sales, number of translations, nor the emotional impact these books would have on children and adults. According to Egmont UK Ltd, which acquired Methuen Publishing's list of children's books, since 1998 it has sold 150,000 to 200,000 original Pooh books per year. Egmont also holds the Disney license for Classic Pooh and on average sells 100,000 copies per year of those books. Averaged to 1926 when *Winnie-the-Pooh* was first published, the total continuous printing would be approaching twenty million books. There have been translations into at least fifty languages, including a *New York Times* best-seller in Latin.

Another artist could have illustrated the stories very differently—with a different sweep of the pen or interpretation of feelings. Fortunately this did not happen. Shepard's exceptional, sensitive illustrations are a big reason the stories have been phenomenal and perennial favorites around the world for generations.

E. H. Shepard's home in the village of Lodsworth

E. H. Shepard's gravestone at the Church of St. Peter in Lodsworth

From "*In Which* Piglet does a very grand thing" (*The House at Pooh Corner*)

The Enduring Legacy of Winnie-the-Pooh

A classic in literature is more than an old book that stays in print. If we think of core books in the children's canon, certain classics come up: *Treasure Island, The Jungle Book, Alice in Wonderland, Peter Pan, The Wind in the Willows,* and *The Secret Garden.* These were written during the Golden Age of children's literature—the late Victorian era to the end of the Edwardian age—and have remained relevant to generations of readers.

It can be difficult to put one's finger on particular elements that help a book stand the test of time. We may all agree that it needs to be well-written. It needs timeless themes and eternal truths. And for children's literature, in particular, it's essential that it pleases two audiences: children must read and re-read the book, and adults must buy it again and again. (And adults must enjoy reading it aloud, over and over and over.)

From the outset, A. A. Milne's and E. H. Shepard's collaborations were a phenomenal commercial success, and in the ninety years since they were published, *Winnie-the-Pooh* and *The House at Pooh Corner* have become such staples of childhood that for many, it may be hard to imagine childhood without them. That you hold this book in your hands reflects a continued fascination with the special physical, literary, and emotional geography of these books.

In a 2014 YouGov poll of two thousand adults in England, *Winnie-the-Pooh* was named as the favorite children's book of the past 150 years. Parents and teachers around the world continue to read Milne's stories and poems aloud to their children and students. In Australia, Margaret Crouch, a teacher in Victor Harbor, read the stories from the Hundred Acre Wood to five- to seven-year-olds for more than a decade. "The best thing I liked about reading them A. A. Milne was seeing the children's reactions on their faces and their enjoyment from the stories. He wrote in such a way that children can easily put themselves in a character's perspective."

Original manuscript of Milne's "Introduction" to *Winnie-the-Pooh*

Today in the venerable Wren Library at his alma mater Trinity College, Cambridge, Milne's manuscripts attract more visitors than Newton's own annotated copy of *Principia*, to the possible chagrin of the archivists and librarians (and maybe Milne, too, if he knew). The original *Winnie-the-Pooh* and *The House at Pooh Corner* are on display Monday through Friday in the library. They are set in tall wooden cases with glass tops, covered in a protective satin blankets alongside the oldest books in the library collection, the eighth century *Epistles of St. Paul* as well as the thirteenth century Anglo-Norman *Trinity Apocalypse*. Side by side these ancient texts are displayed two humble yellow folders which hold the writing that would immortalize Milne's name in stone monuments. The stories we all know were written in small, distinctive, and near-cryptic handwriting in black ink on unlined white 6 × 8-inch notebook paper, the pages now faded from white to an antiquated beige. The writing shows that Milne thought carefully before putting pen to paper, with only occasional words and phrases blocked out with black curlicues scribbled through them—that is, with the exception of "GON OUT, BACKSON, BISY, BACKSON, C.R." in the story "*In Which* Rabbit Has a Busy Day, and We Learn What Christopher Robin Does in the Mornings." For such few lines, he wrote and rewrote and rearranged the words to get the desired effect of

Top Ten Favorite Children's Books from a 2014 YouGov Poll

1. *Winnie-the-Pooh* by A. A. Milne (1926)

2. *Alice's Adventures in Wonderland* by Lewis Carroll (1865)

3. *The Very Hungry Caterpillar* by Eric Carle (1969)

4. *The Hobbit* by J. R. R. Tolkien (1937)

5. *The Gruffalo* by Julia Donaldson (1999)

6. *Charlie and the Chocolate Factory* by Roald Dahl (1964)

7. *Black Beauty* by Anna Sewell (1877)

8. *Treasure Island* by Robert Louis Stevenson (1883)

9. *The BFG* by Roald Dahl (1982)

10. *The Lion, the Witch and the Wardrobe* by C. S. Lewis (1950)

the misspellings. In the top left pages, rusty imprints of paper clips show nearly a century of time has passed. With tiny tea stains sprinkling the manuscript here and there, we can imagine Milne with a cup-and-saucer set to the side as he wrote.

Shepard was one of last century's best black-and-white illustrators of the Victorian tradition, known as well for bringing fame to Kenneth Grahame's *The Wind in the Willows*. In 1969 when he turned ninety, Shepard donated his pencil sketches for the Winnie-the-Pooh books to the Victoria and Albert Museum (the V&A), the world's greatest museum of art and design, based in London. Childhood illustrations and correspondence were donated to the University of Surrey in Guildford near his studio. Like Milne's stories preserved in the Wren Library at Trinity College, the sketches at the V&A are torn from notebooks Shepard carried into Ashdown Forest when walking with Milne. To view them, an appointment is made, and a security guard meets the researcher at the V&A entrance to lead her on labyrinthine paths to a secret archive deep within the V&A. Archivists and curators will set out boxes and boxes of Shepard's work, carefully preserved on window-mounted archival board paper, on big tables in an expansive room under dim lighting. The occasional security guard will walk by and pause to look at the drawings, the tension in his face easing when he sees the characters who populated his own childhood.

Exploring the
Hundred Acre Wood

ORIGINS
of the
STORIES

"All art is autobiographical; the pearl is the oyster's autobiography," wrote Federico Fellini. This is undoubtedly true of Milne, for whom there was a deep connection between himself and the art. The Hundred Acre Wood, the iconic setting of *Winnie-the-Pooh* and *The House at Pooh Corner*, is a reflection of the writer and his lifelong love of wandering open landscapes. When Milne laced up his boots for a walk in the heather and pine, he ventured into a world of the best kind of literature—the kind rooted in a familiar place.

Hartfield, High Street.

Hartfield High Street, around 1900

The Hundred Acre Wood is based on Ashdown Forest, an area that writer and poet G. K. Chesterton famously called "the place where London ends and England can begin." A former royal hunting forest of about 6,500 acres, Ashdown Forest is ten square miles of heathland and woodlands. It's a place of significant ecological importance, with a fascinating cultural history as well. As we tour the literary and natural history of *Winnie-the-Pooh*, you can see where Milne took his inspiration.

Hartfield Village

In the time that has passed since the stories were read to you, and you have read them to your own children or grandchildren, you may wonder what the village and Hundred Acre Wood looks like now. What did it look like when Milne wrote the stories?

The name Hartfield means "open land frequented by stags." It originates from a combination of the Old English words *heorot* (hart and stag) and *feld* (pasture or open country).

TOP LEFT The way between Cotchford Farm and Hartfield

RIGHT Village pump

With a population of two thousand, Hartfield has retained authenticity as a charming English village. Ashdown Forest is located south of the village. It is still a place of solitude where people can walk half a day without meeting another person. There are no overt signs pronouncing your arrival in Pooh Country. There are no bright lights or billboards, no £1 carnival rides, no inflatable Eeyores, Owls, or Roos rising and falling in dramatic flair. There are no signs marking the dirt lane where Milne lived, nor pub grub with names like "Milne Mash and Peas" or a "Tigger's Extract of Malt Cocktail" on ice. A quiet authenticity—historical, literary, and environmental—has settled over the landscape.

War memorial

LEFT **Village commerce**

TOP RIGHT **Civic pride**

The significant literary, physical, and cultural landscapes have not been exploited. There is a quiet and rugged repose about the place. It is among the best surviving medieval landscapes in Northern Europe, situated within the High Weald Area of Outstanding Natural Beauty (AONB)—meaning, countryside considered to have significant landscape value in England, Wales, or Northern Ireland. As the purpose of the AONB is to conserve and enhance natural beauty, these guardians have prevented the landscape from becoming overrun by Milne memorabilia or Pooh paraphernalia.

Hartfield reflects quintessentially English traditions: pride in Queen Elizabeth's reign and its own status as an award-winning

St. Mary the Virgin Church

TOP LEFT **The Anchor Inn**

RIGHT **Cottage garden**

village. Inasmuch as the famously reserved English are remotely capable of boasting, there are only a few plaques and signs—inconspicuous, but look closely as you walk about—reflecting these highly coveted awards of English civic pride. At the entrances to the village, handsome iron signs with "Hartfield 1952–2002" are painted in gold to mark the Queen's Golden Jubilee. Intermingled on the High Street and side streets are quaint two-story cottages, black-and-white timber and plaster Tudor homes, pubs, and a couple shops. On a row of whitewashed cottages with doors the color of Easter eggs and names like Primrose Cottage, a demure red-and-brown plaque reads, "Best Kept Small Village 1974." Civic pride busted free, as nearly twenty years later, a new and bigger plaque— "Best Kept Village in All Sussex 1991"—is on full, glorious display at the village park near the village pump.

Just up the lane from the pump is the church and cemetery. On the other side of town are the earthen remains of an old castle. In summer months, a tiny park the size of a postage stamp overflows with blooming plants, and little girls with names of flowers play in polka-dotted dresses. "Three, two, one! Rose, here I come!" Geraniums, verbena, and roses surround the memorial to village men who fought in World Wars I and II. Mellifluous thrushes, robins, and other birds fill the leafy village with song at dawn and dusk. Friends and strangers, cricket players, and other like-minded souls receive warm welcomes at the two village pubs: the fifteenth-century Anchor Inn and sixteenth-century Haywaggon. Ales, lagers, ciders, and pub food are served in gardens or indoors, where low-beamed ceilings, hearths, and snugs give refuge to travelers, the nice fellow who alternates between pubs in Withyham and Hartfield, and

OVERLEAF **Frothy
fields of rapeseed
near Hartfield**

Summer flowers in the village

RIGHT **Celtic cross headstone in cemetery of St. Mary the Virgin Church**

OPPOSITE **From "*In Which Christopher Robin Leads an Expotition to the North Pole*" (*Winnie-the-Pooh*)**

cricket players who have just come off the village green. Nearby are the village hall, old castle earth mounds, and a train station with remnants of a former platform. The town croft where the Hartfield and Withyham cricket clubs compete is an open space on high ground and home to a grand old oak worth seeking out. The cricket rivals share cucumber sandwiches and Victoria sponge cake in the clubhouse, then head to the Anchor Inn for a pint of Harveys ale.

So little has changed or stands out in Hartfield since the Hundred Acre Wood was created. The only indications of Milne's presence are a shop called Pooh Corner and the modest signpost pointing to the footpath to Poohsticks Bridge. This subtlety reflects an ethos of conservation of the literary and natural landscapes.

And so it is within this well-preserved village and surrounding ancient landscape that we embark on our exploration of the Hundred Acre Wood. But—*think, think, think*—where to start first? We could begin with a cup of tea in the village, by counting trees in the Enchanted Place, or even racing twigs in the lazy river currents at Poohsticks Bridge.

But why not start at the place where the stories originated? That would be Cotchford Farm. From his bedroom study there, Milne would walk downstairs to the hearth in the sitting room, where he read aloud drafts of the stories to his wife and son. We will first tour the house and garden, and I will tell you stories about this place and that place which influenced the stories. We can then go on an Expotition and amble down Jib Jacks Hill to Hartfield and then farther afield. I've put some Provisions together—a thermos of tea and a little smackerel of something. You just need a waterproof hat, waterproof boots, and a waterproof macintosh.

This is England, after all.

Christopher Robin was sitting outside his door, putting on his Big Boots. As soon as he saw the Big Boots, Pooh knew that an Adventure was going to happen, and he brushed the honey off his nose with the back of his paw, and spruced himself up as well as he could, so as to look Ready for Anything.

—A. A. Milne, "*In Which* Christopher Robin
Leads an Expotition to the North Pole,"
Winnie-the-Pooh

Cotchford Farm

Christopher Robin's childhood home still enchants millions of people all over the world. The twenty stories in *Winnie-the-Pooh* and *The House at Pooh Corner* were inspired by several real places including Posingford Wood, Ashdown Forest, and the Five Hundred Acre Wood, but the idea for the tales originated at Cotchford Farm, a place still as serene, atmospheric, and beautiful as when the Milne family lived there. Far older than Daphne's Brooklands on the Hamble, Cotchford Farm is, as the name implies, an old English farm—unpretentious and comfortable, a former working farm. It is unlike an English "country home" in the classic estate sense of long avenues, grand proportions, hunting and shooting grounds, and Palladian architecture. The famous English landscape designer Capability Brown did not shift any earth here. There are special places here which Milne wove into the settings of his stories. Can you guess which stories could have originated here at the farm? The Heffalump Trap? Pooh's Thoughtful Spot? Eeyore's Gloomy Place? You may delight in finding the answers.

Before the family permanently moved to Cotchford Farm from London, they were half-countrymen, visiting on weekends, Easter, and summer holidays. Located about a mile southwest of the Hartfield parish church, Cotchford Farm was absolutely loved by the Milnes. It took possession of them when they took possession of it in 1925, Christopher Robin recalled in his autobiography, *The Enchanted Places*.

With their chauffeur, Mr. Burnside, at the wheel, they made weekly journeys from London in their classic blue Fiat, arriving Saturday morning and leaving Monday afternoon. Christopher and Nanny sat in the front seat. His mother and father sat in back. The roadster motored through Hartfield, passing little shops and cottages with pastel doors, and at a fork in the road where a magnificent 300-year-old oak stands, turned left onto Jib Jacks Hill. They drove uphill half a mile, and then drove downhill for another half a mile. The most exciting moment of the journey, as Christopher

It is my house, and I built it where I said I did, so the wind must have blown it here. And the wind blew it right over the wood, and blew it down here, and here it is as good as ever. In fact, better in places.

—Eeyore, "*In Which* a House Is Built at Pooh Corner for Eeyore,"
The House at Pooh Corner

Robin remembered, was when the car slowed for a turn as they approached the dirt lane leading to Cotchford Farm. He remembered how the "smooth motion changed into the familiar, welcoming, beloved bumping. For the lane was no more than a sandy track, well rutted by the wooden, iron-rimmed wheels of farm carts." The ruts filled with rainwater in the winter, creating big splashes. "I loved it. It was just how it should be: a proper country lane." The ruts and bumps still mercilessly come and go. By winter's end, the short journey from the paved road to Cotchford Farm is still a jolting experience. Daphne and Milne liked it this way: the bumpier the better. That would discourage people from building houses along it or seeking out the celebrity author.

After the bumpity bumps, Burnside turned left down a steep gravel driveway into Cotchford Farm. Pheasants greeted them with their metallic squawks from the asparagus patch. Burnside would turn around and drive back to London, returning Monday afternoon to pick them up. If they wanted to get around other than by foot, Milne would call up George Mitchell in Upper Hartfield. He ran a car repair and part-time taxi business. Milne didn't drive for another few years, so Mitchell would pick up Milne or Daphne in his 1925 Daimler Silent Knight with its partition and speaker, and drive them anywhere they needed to go. "One time, Milne needed a ride, but my father explained to him that mother was returning from the hospital. I had just been born," explained Mitchell's son, Tom. "My father said Milne didn't mind. So my first ride home from the hospital was with A. A. Milne in the car."

Cotchford farmhouse

Hearing their car, the Milnes' full-time gardener George Tasker would emerge from the greenhouse in his customary collar, tie, and brown homburg hat.

"Good morning, Tasker."

"Good morning, Sir. And good morning, Madam."

Tasker and Milne were comrades beyond the garden. "A swarthy bloke, a bloody good-looking fellow," according to his son, Peter, Tasker had served in World War I like Milne and was awarded a Silver Wound Badge after lying wounded on the battlefield during the Battle of the Somme. When he returned to Hartfield, his days were spent tending vegetables and flowers as Milne's professional full-time gardener for £3 per week. He headed the local horticultural society and grew award-winning chrysanthemums in the

Cotchford greenhouse, taking his best each spring to the Chelsea Flower Show. When Peter was born in 1930, Milne gave Tasker a Winnie-the-Pooh teddy bear. Growing up, Peter frequently helped his father in the Cotchford garden. He recalled, "My father used to have the fire on all the time in the greenhouse. In the summer, he used to put these chrysanths in the open air. And he used to cut all the buds off except one so it would blossom. My job was to wheel them in at night." Peter remembers that Milne was reserved but engaged, listening for hours in the garden and sitting room as Peter recalled his time as a Royal Marine in the Korean War.

Inside and out, the Milnes' former home and gardens feel comfortable and enveloping, long settled in their place. With gentle roof lines and a mixture of tiles, brickwork, and stone, and alterations made throughout the centuries, the farmhouse has an unpretentious appeal. The farmhouse sits on a leveled section of a leafy hill slope.

Originally built around 1550, the farmhouse is, like many old English homes, a complex sequence of additions and developments. The ivy- and wisteria-covered house we see today started life as one cottage—a small two-cell dwelling. The early seventeenth century was a period of enhancing the social status of the house with a new wing set at a right angle to the old building. At two and a half stories, it forms the main part of the house seen today. In the small courtyard entrance to the front door, a haunting water cistern from 1780 serves both as a reminder of passing time and as a functional planter overflowing with snapdragons, salvias, and petunias. In an unintended nod to Daphne Milne, this area fills with the sweet, heady fragrance of *Daphne odora* 'Aureomarginata'. Planted near the front door, it has clusters of late winter and early spring white flowers, evoking a pleasant reverie of Daphne Milne, the former lady of the home, lingering in her beloved gardens while her son plays outside and her husband writes upstairs.

From early twentieth-century photographs, the landscape surrounding the house appears undomesticated and uncultivated.

When royalties started coming in from the Winnie-the-Pooh books, Daphne enlisted the help of a local landscape architect named Mr. Berrow. He designed a terraced garden sympathetic to the sloping landscape, with long stone pathways extending south across the garden. A circular garden was filled roses, another specialty of their gardener. The landscape took shape, and, poring over catalogues and books by popular 1920s garden writer Marion Cran, Daphne filled the garden with herbaceous perennials. There were colorful borders of azaleas reminiscent of those from Daphne's childhood home, Brooklands. She and Tasker planted hundreds of Darwin tulips throughout the garden. The garden burst with purple and plum-colored penstemons, waves of perfumed, jewel-box phlox, and shimmering heleniums at high summer. Drifts of striking bergamots and rudbeckias attracted bees and butterflies. Dahlias reminded Milne of his mother and the ones she grew under his bedroom window. When journalists came to meet the famous writer and catch a peek of the very, very shy Christopher Robin, they would always, he later recalled, win the favor of his mother if they complimented her flower arrangements and gardens. He remembers his mother happily and quietly pottering in the garden in the daylight and the dusk, brooding over her plants in happy self-companionship. He was welcomed into this natural world. She taught him the names of flowers like *Salpiglossis* and *Spiraea* as well as the tongue-twisting *Eschscholtzia*. Listening to his five-year-old try to pronounce the Latin names of plants surely gave Milne some comic inspiration.

"Christopher Robin gave me a mastershalum seed, and I planted it, and I'm going to have mastershalums all over the front door."

"I thought they were called nasturtiums," said Piglet timidly, as he went on jumping.

"No," said Pooh. "Not these. These are called mastershalums."

—From "*In Which* It Is Shown Tiggers Don't Climb Trees," *The House at Pooh Corner*

An eighteenth-century cistern at the entrance to Cotchford Farm

Milne was someone who liked to go on proper walks in the country—a walk with purpose, preferably. He was happiest playing ball games: putting, golf, cricket, and catch. After a meal, the garden was also where he went in search of a shady area, and, "armed with deck chair, cushions, rugs and pullovers, retired there to reverberate gently until tea time," as his son remembers.

Among the first things Milne did when they bought the farm was lay out a clock golf course on the only lawn the property possessed. Cricket and catch were played in the meadow. When his father wasn't around, Christopher Robin threw the ball against a wall which is still in the garden. Running through the orchard north of the house was a straight level bit of the garden. It was a grass path five feet wide and twenty yards long. This was the first "pitch" (or "field," if you are an American reader) where father would bowl (or "pitch"!) soft tennis balls to his son in his first games of cricket. Nanny was also enlisted in the games. Lifting her uniform dress above her shoes, she chased balls up and down the slope and beyond the boundaries of the orchard—perhaps wondering at the same time if her job description included such activity! When Tasker later built a proper pitch with a net, she undoubtedly sighed in relief. Tasker's son, Peter, was ten years younger than Christopher Robin and remembers years of cricket with him. "When I was about fourteen or fifteen, I used to bowl cricket balls to him. He'd been away at college and came back to play for Hartfield."

Inside the farmhouse, three floors with several landings and mezzanines from centuries of construction might confuse the visitor, but they gave Christopher Robin myriad secret crawl spaces. From stripped oak paneling and rough-hewn beams, it looks like creatures from the Hundred Acre Wood leapt from the pages to nibble the wood. And where did Milne create these characters? He wrote in a couple of places. As they didn't have electricity except in Daphne's room, nor believed in central heating, they lit the house with candles and relied on three fireplaces for warmth in a very countrified way. In the winter, he wrote in a small space near the hearth in the drawing room. When Brian Jones of The Rolling Stones lived here, he painted the ceilings between wood beams a bright blue, which has since been restored to white. The walls to Milne's former writing room have since been removed to make the

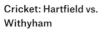

Cricket: Hartfield vs. Withyham

Daphne, Christopher Robin, and Milne at Cotchford Farm with sycamore in background

drawing room more expansive. In warmer months, he wrote upstairs on the first floor in a cheerful bedroom study with five south-facing windows. Other times he wrote in London.

Five yards from Milne's window was a mature sycamore. They are hardy and robust trees, magnificently thick-trunked, and can grow to be taller than a hundred feet. They can also live four hundred years. This one was planted between 1810 and 1850 judging by its size in historical photographs. Its elegant canopy cast dappled shade over the three-story farmhouse, leaves emerging crimson and turning green in the spring. We can imagine the pleasure Milne took looking up from his writing desk, perhaps remembering the wildflowers with which H. G. Wells enlivened lectures on botany, perhaps remembering tree-climbing in Hampstead Heath with Ken.

Through the window, he saw the changing moods of the tree: in spring, green-yellow flowers hanging in narrow racemes, and in autumn when leaves turned yellow, winged seeds twirling to earth. When Christopher Robin was young, and the wind rustled the sycamore's leaves near his bedroom windows, the sound terrified him.

In the books, the fictional Christopher Robin's house is introduced in the first chapter when Pooh, hearing the buzzing of bees and perpetually in search of honey, climbs a tree. He falls out and enlists the help of Christopher Robin. Shepard rendered Christopher Robin's home as an enormous tree with green and yellow leaves. After reviewing Shepard's initial drawing of the Hundred

Acre Wood, Milne asked for all trees to have doors in them, and so a green wooden door opens into Christopher Robin's tree house. We can make out the shadows of things hanging inside the house. A small window provides a view of the forest. For Milne, with his writing desk perched high in the tree branches, that tree was an important inkwell of inspiration for creating the tree houses of Owl, Piglet, and Christopher Robin.

Drawing from real life, Shepard captured the sycamore and the meadow, as well as the only depiction of Cotchford farmhouse, in the illustration to the poem "Buttercups Days." Here Christopher Robin and Anne, his childhood playmate, both in their bobbed haircuts and checkered smocks, pick wildflower bouquets, the tree casting dappled light near Milne's upstairs bedroom-study and capturing the inspiring panorama of gardens, meadows, and forest upon which Milne looked while writing.

Cotchford Farm in "Buttercup Days" (*Now We Are Six*)

The garden sundial with its cavalcade of characters from the Hundred Acre Wood

LEFT Christopher Robin watches over the garden at Cotchford Farm.

While iconic trees have come and gone, Milne history still saturates the gardens. The wall where Christopher used to throw his ball still stands. Between the house and the river is the meadow where he and his father used to play cricket with each other, returning to the house to find a jug of lemonade waiting for them in the dining room. The mossy pedestal of a sundial is carved with creatures from the Hundred Acre Wood, and the face of it reads, "This warm and sunny spot belongs to Pooh, and here he wonders what it's time to do."

Pooh's House from *"In Which* We Are Introduced to Winnie-the-Pooh and Some Bees, and the Stories Begin" (*Winnie-the-Pooh*)

Pooh's House

Entrances should entrance. From garden gates to opening lines in a book, openings should take readers and garden visitors into new worlds. They draw us in and take us on new journeys of the mind. Gardeners do this with visual and sensual artistry: mystery around corners and plants which pique our senses.

Unlike the static printed words in a book, gardens are living, breathing landscapes which change over time. Milne's original words and stories are constant, unchanging, fixed on paper, but the gardens, forest, and woods that inspired the setting have changed over time. If you were a guest at Cotchford Farm in the 1920s, you would have had a different experience than if you visit now. Trees Daphne planted are approaching the century mark. Her rose gardens are gone. Some paths and terraces remain.

A key feature at the entrance to Cotchford Farm was an old walnut tree. It stood for more than two hundred years, and though the last of it came down in the early 1970s, it lives on through literature. This tree—which was either an English walnut or a black walnut—is historically significant as it was the catalyst for all the stories we've grown to love. As Christopher Robin wrote, "Posingford, the Forest, the Five Hundred Acre: this was where it all happened, but not where it started. It started much nearer to home: at the top of the garden, in an ancient walnut tree." (Depending on your measuring stick, an ancient tree might be five hundred years old, but, for a walnut, two to three hundred years is considered old.)

This tree was a handsome specimen, a thick sentry at the top of the driveway at Cotchford Farm. Planted between 1670 and 1770, it provided nuts for eating and limbs for climbing on. At its maturity, it would have been nearly one hundred feet tall, its shady canopy stretching across the entrance to the house. By the 1920s, the tree was in decline. It developed what old trees often do—a hollow cavity in its trunk. This fissure may have been the result of stress from natural forces—wind, fire, heat, lightning, rain, insect attacks, bacteria, or fungi—any of which could result in the exposure of the heartwood.

Whatever the reason, there it was—a big tree with a great gash in its trunk. What might a child think? What would *you* have thought as a child? Irresistible! For five-year-old Christopher Robin, it offered a magical hideaway. A small, dark, enclosed space appeals to children, as the world around them can seem very big. Tree hollows and tree houses, tents, teepees, and forts—nooks and crannies such as these provide opportunities for children to retreat and create imaginary worlds away from the watchful eyes of parents. These holes and houses feel safe, like cozy nests. What child hasn't created a home out of sticks outside or blankets under a table? And what adult doesn't remember doing the same?

Of the innumerable charms of *Winnie-the-Pooh* and *The House at Pooh Corner*, one of the most appealing is the rendering of

Good bone structure in a similar 200-year-old black walnut tree

animal homes in hollows and burrows. Think of the homes of Owl, Pooh, Piglet, Rabbit, and Kanga. These small, tight spaces are so tempting and so fascinating to children. In creating these, Milne tapped into the desire of very young children to have their own secret hideaways, close to—but far enough away from—the watchful eyes of parents. Milne's little boy spent so much time in trees—mostly in apples and hazels—and this amused and inspired the father and the writer who enjoyed the same hideaways in Hampstead Heath and other parks and places in England with his brother. He lived nostalgically through his son.

To Christopher Robin, it was the perfect tree house: he could climb inside the tree and look high above his head at the canopy of green leaves and blue sky. He could sit on the soft, cool floor of

Christopher Robin with
Pooh, Piglet, and Roo in
the original walnut tree

decayed wood bark and arrange curios inside on natural ledges and hooks. Reflecting on it as an adult, he said: "Pooh and I claimed it. It was Pooh's House, really, but there was plenty of room for us both inside, and here we came to play our small, quiet, happy games together." The tree made its debut in chapter one of *Winnie-the-Pooh*, where, sitting on a log in front of a fire, a bell-ringer over his furry right shoulder, is Pooh. What a life for any tree: a long-lived provider of food, beauty, play, and shade, as well as the origin of what many would regard as one of the greatest children's books.

The Trap for Heffalumps

At Cotchford Farm, the old walnut tree provided enough room for the real Christopher Robin and his stuffed bear, but when his London friend Anne came to visit the country, the hollow felt crowded. Anne could visit, of course. She could come for tea. But living there? Utterly impossible, recalled Christopher Robin in his autobiography. Children of this age do not easily give up their space, even to best friends. Fortunately there was another piece of real estate close by—the well house, a shelter which covered over a new well dug to supply the Taskers' cottage. The underground well was enclosed and a wooden shed covered it. Playing neighbors, Christopher Robin and Anne "visited" each other by walking along a path he had made.

From *"In Which* Piglet Meets a Heffalump*"
(*Winnie-the-Pooh*)

The little stone path had been inspired by a garden project that was underway at the time. A man named Mr. Farmer had been hired to build crazy paving through their rock garden. Christopher Robin loved to watch him set down the sand base, arrange stones in patterns on top, and brush and water sand into the spaces between them. He wanted to do it, too. Mr. Farmer let him choose smaller stones, which Christopher Robin then carried one by one to his own "home" and garden under the walnut tree. There he laid his own path from the tree to the pump shed where Anne "lived." Tasker then created a wooden sundial for him. But in the child's mind, there was a problem: having an eye-catching object like a sundial was now a concern. He was afraid trespassers with malicious intent could sneak down the path and steal the sundial or some other precious thing inside his walnut tree house. So what would any child do to capture a thief? "I dug a heffalump trap at the other end and carefully disguised it with sticks and grass."

Unfortunately, he snagged something else. "I caught Mrs. Tasker's foot."

Christopher Robin's camouflaged trap—and the capture of the gardener's wife's ankle as she retrieved water from the pump—inspired Milne to write the story "Piglet Meets a Heffalump." Rendered as an Indian elephant by Shepard, Heffalumps were so named by a child trying to pronounce the name of the elephants he saw at the London Zoo with Nanny. Perhaps a Heffalump Trap was his attempt not only to capture trespassers, but also to overcome his own fears about the animal in real life.

In the story, Christopher Robin, Pooh, and Piglet are all talking together on a patch of summer grass. It is somewhere in the forest. A blanket is spread with plates, picnic nibbles, and a pot of honey. Christopher Robin carelessly says, "I saw a Heffalump today, Piglet." That neither Piglet nor Pooh even know what a Heffalump really looks like is beside the point. Once the picnic is over, Piglet and Pooh hatch a plan. As they approach the Six Pine Trees, they decide there is an adventure to be had.

> Pooh looked round to see that Nobody else was listening, and said in a very solemn voice:
>
> "Piglet, I have decided something."
>
> "What have you decided, Pooh?"
>
> "I have decided to catch a Heffalump."
>
> Pooh nodded his head several times as he said this, and waited for Piglet to say "How?" or "Pooh, you couldn't!" or something helpful of that sort, but Piglet said nothing. The fact was Piglet was wishing that he had thought about it first.
>
> "I shall do it," Pooh said, after waiting a little longer, "by means of a trap. And it must be a cunning trap, so you will have to help me, Piglet."

Silly conversations between Pooh and Piglet follow, as they plot ways to bravely capture Heffalumps. They decide honey is much more a trappy thing than Piglet's food, haycorns. Pooh gets the honey while Piglet digs a Very Deep Pit. They decide to meet at six o'clock the next morning by the Six Pine Trees.

But during the night, Pooh and Piglet both wake up. Pooh's concerns are pedestrian. He is hungry and his only pot of honey is sitting as bait at the bottom of a Cunning Trap. He needs to take his mind off of it. He tries counting sheep. He tries counting Heffalumps. He can bear it no longer! He runs out of his house to the Six Pine Trees. Milne sets the scene: "The Sun was still in bed, but there was still a lightness in the sky over the Hundred Acre Wood which seemed to show that it was waking up and would soon be kicking off the clothes."

To no one's surprise, Pooh winds up down at the bottom of the Cunning Trap with the honey. At the same time, Piglet awakes and wonders: What was a Heffalump like? Was it Fierce? *Did* it come when you whistled? And *how* did it come? Was it Fond of Pigs at all? If it was Fond of pigs, did it make any difference *what sort* of Pig?

Winnie-the-Pooh's relationship with honey is not complicated, from "*In Which* Piglet Meets a Heffalump" (*Winnie-the-Pooh*)

Little Piglet wants to face down his fears. He marches to the Heffalump Trap. He creeps to the side and peers in. But, in Pooh's effort to lick every last bit of honey, he has gotten his head stuck in the jar. At the moment Piglet looks down, Pooh is making loud roaring noises, stumbling, and bumping his head on tree roots. Horrified, Piglet cries and scampers to Christopher Robin, who discovers the Heffalump in the Cunning Trap is actually Pooh, whose head has just hit a root and smashed the jar.

Like all stories in the Hundred Acre Wood, this one was inspired by real places and people, fears and joys, and stirred by a father's writerly imagination. Christopher Robin did dig a Heffalump trap near the walnut tree at Cotchford Farm. In the story "Piglet Meets a Heffalump," the trap is situated near the Six Pine Trees. Those six pines could have been anywhere in Ashdown Forest, and the Heffalump Trap is a touching, silly story of pluck and bravery—perhaps a father's gentle way of encouraging his son to face his own fears.

Piglet dreaming, from *"In Which Piglet meets a Heffalump"* (*Winnie-the-Pooh*)

**Rounding the spinney, from
"*In Which* Pooh and Piglet Go
Hunting and Nearly Catch a
Woozle" (*Winnie-the-Pooh*)**

Where the Woozle Wasn't

One fine winter day in the book *Winnie-the-Pooh,* we meet Piglet, a Very Small Animal and Pooh's closest friend, for the first time. Piglet is brushing the snow from the front of his house and looks up. There is his friend Winnie-the-Pooh, walking around and around in circles.

"Hallo!" said Piglet, "what are you doing?"

"Hunting," said Pooh.

"Hunting what?"

"Tracking something," said Winnie-the-Pooh very mysteriously.

"Tracking what?" said Piglet, coming closer.

"That's just what I ask myself. I ask myself, What?"

"What do you think you'll answer?"

"I shall have to wait until I catch up with it," said Winnie-the-Pooh. "Now look there." He pointed to the ground in front of him. "What do you see there?"

"Tracks," said Piglet. "Paw-marks." He gave a little squeak of excitement. "Oh, Pooh! Do you think it's a-a-a Woozle?"

There's a mystery. There's nothing to do until Friday. The best friends Pooh and Piglet set off on an adventure into the woods. We learn in the story how Piglet is timid yet excitable, though he tries to be brave and occasionally conquer his fears. They walk along. Pooh looks down in the snow and notices that there are actually two animals following them. "Look!"

"What?" said Piglet, with a jump. And then, to show that he hadn't been frightened, he jumped up and down once or twice more in an exercising sort of way.

"The tracks!" said Pooh. *"A third animal has joined the other two!"*

"Pooh!" cried Piglet. "Do you think it is another Woozle?"

Examining Woozle
tracks, from "*In Which
Pooh and Piglet Go
Hunting and Nearly
Catch a Woozle*"
(*Winnie-the-Pooh*)

The friends now both feel anxious. They are afraid that the three animals tromping in the snow ahead of them are of Hostile Intent. Piglet pines for his grandfather Trespassers W, and Pooh hopes they might "suddenly but quite accidentally" run into Christopher Robin. They then look down again and find four tracks in the trail. Pooh licks the tip of his nose; never has he been more frightened. These Woozle tracks are crossing over each other now. Piglet, always a little anxious but now more so than ever, decides he has somewhere else to be, now, and races home.

Christopher Robin whistles from an oak tree, from *"In Which* Pooh and Piglet Go Hunting and Nearly Catch a Woozle" (*Winnie-the-Pooh*)

Above him comes a whistle. It is Christopher Robin. He has been sitting on the branch of a big oak tree, watching the adventure unfold. "Silly old Bear," he says, and tells Pooh how he has watched him go around the spinney twice alone and then together with Piglet and then was about ready to go for a fourth round. Pooh realizes he and Piglet have been following their own tracks in search of Grandfathers or Woozles or Wizzles.

Can we align the story with a real place? Maybe yes, maybe no. In the story, Milne writes that there is a "small spinney of larch-trees" here, but doesn't situate it anywhere specific. Shepard doesn't render the spinney—a small wood or copse—as one surrounded by heather or gorse from Ashdown Forest. In the

illustrations, it is suggested to be a thicket of arching trees, probably hazel. It could be anywhere there are spinneys—perhaps Posingford Wood or the Five Hundred Acre Wood. We know that Milne took Shepard on a walk in Ashdown Forest through Posingford Wood and over Poohsticks Bridge to the heathland. As photographs of Ashdown Forest in the 1920s show, the land there was barren of trees with the exception of occasional oaks and clumps of tall Scots pine.

The current owner of Cotchford Farm has suggested that the spinney near the farmhouse—a little wood of arching hazel, crooked birch, stout pine, and a maple or two—could have provided inspiration for Milne. It looks to be a remnant from the past, a little wood that hasn't been cut down for either meadow or garden. We can imagine Milne looking out his writing window, seeing his curious little boy walking around the spinney, and creating a story from the delightful scene of a boy caught up in his own imaginative landscape.

A Floody Place

Wind, rain, mist, sun, and snow: when different weather moods transformed Ashdown Forest, they also saturated, dried out, and blew through the Hundred Acre Wood. To the young Christopher Robin, rain in the country seemed wholly different from rain in London. At Cotchford Farm, the water sculpted the river bed in intricate and magical new ways. When the little Christopher Robin grew up, he also recalled how, in his father's stories, the real and fictional Christopher Robin blended together and the activities and fascinations are inseparable. This is particularly illustrated in chapter nine of *Winnie-the-Pooh*, entitled "*In Which* Piglet Is Entirely Surrounded by Water."

Escaping with pots of honey, from *"In Which* Piglet Is Entirely Surrounded by Water" (*Winnie-the-Pooh*)

The little dry ditches in which Piglet had nosed about so often had become streams, the little streams across which he had splashed were rivers, and the river, between whose steep banks they had played so happily, had sprawled out of its own bed and was taking up so much room that Piglet was beginning to wonder whether it would be coming into *his* bed soon.

In this story about rain, Piglet is a Very Small Animal Entirely Surrounded by Water, and quite Anxious as well. He wishes he was in Pooh's house, Christopher Robin's house, or Rabbit's house, anywhere but his own house as it is entirely surrounded by water. In hopes of a rescue, he tosses a message in a bottle—"HELP! PIGLIT (ME)"—into the rising waters and hopes it reaches someone who can perform a rescue.

At times such as this, both Christopher Robins put on their Wellington boots and macintoshes and, venturing to the edge of the rising tide, poked sticks into the ground to mark the water. Milne observed his own son watch rising flood water from his nursery windows and created a story out of it. Located at the bottom of a hill, Cotchford Farm transformed into a liquid landscape when, across the meadow, the peaceful brown stream became a river. It would race and swirl and froth into something new. It would inch toward the house and eventually seep into the stories, becoming a featured character. Milne watched his son playing, perhaps with sentimental and paternal eyes in remembrance of his own boyhood in the country. The water never reached the house, though the meadow became a lake and Daphne's rose garden and mauve garden receded under the flood. Christopher Robin later noted that those who built Cotchford in the valley had observed the water line over time and, knowing the river's temperament, sited the house's foundation eighteen inches above the water's highest point. Especially during English winters, Cotchford Farm could be a Floody Place, but Cotchford farmhouse was never a Floody House.

Back in his own house, Pooh has fallen asleep in his chair after a tiring Expotition to find the East Pole. With water all around him, he jolts awake and splashes to his front door with pots of honey. Sitting on a big branch, emptying his honey jars for a few days, he sees Piglet's message-in-a-bottle float by. Exclaiming, "Honey!" Pooh plunges into the water in a tubby bear belly-flop, grabs hold of the bottle, and wrestles it up to his branch. He realizes this is not a pot of the golden elixir but could substitute as a boat. He dubs it *The Floating Bear* and, in some of the most comic illustrations of the book, wrestles with the jar, flipping over and over, in and out of the water, finally becoming captain of his new "boat."

In his own house at the top of the forest, the storybook Christopher Robin is warm and dry. He likes being on top of a hill, we hear him think, and it feels jolly to see water surrounding him. It rains and rains, but he stays dry, measuring the rising levels outside his house every day with a stick. On the fifth day of rain, he realizes he is on an island. Owl swoops in. Piglet's message floats by. Piglet must be rescued, they realize. As we readers know, Christopher Robin's umbrella becomes another boat, christened *The Brain of Pooh* (Captain, C. Robin; First Mate, P. Bear), which swirls and bobs in the water until it reaches Piglet, stranded both by water and by Owl's typically long-winded story about his aunt who laid a seagull egg by mistake. All ends well in the story because Christopher Robin comes to the rescue.

Marking the water line, from "*In Which* Piglet Is Entirely Surrounded by Water" (*Winnie-the-Pooh*)

Eeyore's Gloomy Place

From beloved blankets to threadbare stuffed animals, children—in Western cultures especially—carry and caress soft objects for comfort and play. As adults, we treasure the memories of our own soft lovies tucked under our chins at bedtime, the silk edging of a blanket that gave us comfort when sad or lonely, the downy teddy bear who seemed to be more than an imaginary friend. When our own mothers' arms weren't available to hold us, these things soothed and reassured us, providing a bridge to the external world beyond her embrace.

These small and humble transitional objects are links between mother and the real world and have great significance. Some of us wrap our bridal bouquets in our childhood blankets, others take our fuzzy friends with us to university, some go to the grave with them. But at the beginning of our lives, when we cling to our mothers like monkeys, much care is often taken by parents, grandparents, and other loved ones to select or hand-make blankets or animals for young children to clutch. And yet, for mysterious reasons, children make up their own minds about what pleases and placates them, rejecting one thing for another. These particularities explain many an anxious car ride home to retrieve a forgotten doll or blanket when no substitution will suffice. Part of the charm and longevity of Milne's books is seeing the stuffed animals we may remember juxtaposed against a real forest backdrop of gorse, heather, and pines. It re-opens that magical, imaginary world we remember, a twilight time between dependence and independence.

As children are wont to do, Christopher Robin shaped the appearance of the soft animals in his nursery through his caresses and cuddles. Over time, charming bends and twists in their features came from clutching them by the foot or curling them under his arms. Their form shaped the way Milne fashioned their characters. It also shaped how Shepard drew them. This is especially so with the character Eeyore. We are introduced to the downcast donkey in the story *"In Which* Eeyore Loses a Tail and Pooh Finds One"

Eeyore feels a little low, from *"In Which* Eeyore Has a
Birthday and Gets Two Presents" (*Winnie-the-Pooh*)

from the first book, *Winnie-the-Pooh*. With his depressed demeanor, Eeyore has a melancholy and overcast air about him. As he stands alone under a tree or covered in snow wondering where his house went, his long ears flop uncontrollably into his face. Shepard's rendering implies the poor donkey cannot even control the fate of these appendages or see the world clearly through them.

In this particular chapter, Pooh has come along and senses there is something wrong with Eeyore. Whether he is standing alone looking at himself in a stream or munching on thistles, Eeyore exudes gloom and pessimism and the sense that he is crumpled by the weight of life. Sunny days feel cloudy to him. His whole demeanor suggests life is hard. The donkey reveals he hasn't felt right for a long time.

"Dear, dear," said Pooh. "I'm sorry about that. Let's have a look at you."

After examining Eeyore in a circumspect manner, Pooh comes to the conclusion that something is indeed wrong! Something has gone missing! And it concerns the back end of Eeyore—his tail. On a patch of green grass near a prickly gorse shrub, Eeyore slowly turns in one direction, then another, and looks between his legs to get a good look at his back end. Eeyore's tail, he confirms, is gone.

"Somebody must have taken it," he says. "You're a real friend," says he. "Not like some."

Pooh sets off to find it in the Hundred Acre Wood and meets up with Owl.

Many of the stuffed animals and farm animals, including a donkey like Eeyore, came into the life of the real Christopher Robin when the Milne family moved to Cotchford Farm. A pet donkey was named Jessica. There were two fox terriers who in short time proved mistakes and were duly replaced with cats. A tortoiseshell cat with two names, Pinkle and Tattoo, roamed the farm with generations of her progeny casting haughty glances over their shoulders at the Milne family and their guests. As Daphne and Milne wanted their son to have a childhood much like their own, with rich nature encounters, freedom to roam, and trees to climb, real and imaginary companions were important. His stuffed animals were also his dear playmates as a young child (though he set them aside—in a glass cabinet—when he went to boarding school). He also played and fished with William Sackville, the tenth Earl De La Warr, at nearby Buckhurst. For an only child, shy and introspective, a lively country life with an assortment of creatures was important, his parents felt. Christopher Robin also collected frog spawn in jam jars on windowsills, built homes for hedgehogs, and set out cheese for mice who crawled through a hole in his bedroom wall.

For many years, Jessica the donkey was kept in a pasture in the meadow between the farmhouse and the river. It was Nanny's job to retrieve her for rides. And if the donkey acted in an obstinate manner, Tasker was summoned to help. Of course, this pasture is an easy place to pinpoint as the original inspiration for "Eeyore's Gloomy Place." In some ways, the characteristics of the landscape here mirror the dark and swampy place where the fictional Eeyore lived. In fact, in E. H. Shepard's beautiful preparatory drawing of the master plan of the Hundred Acre Wood (pages 8–9), the label that eventually read "Eeyore's Gloomy Place" was "Eeyore's Pasture Land." What could be more obvious than this pasture as the origins for Eeyore's Gloomy Place?

This is one place in the Hundred Acre Wood that can be more complicated than others. If pressed, the adult Christopher Robin felt that this pasture was likely the original inspiration for the gloomy place. Others like to say it was situated in Wrens Warren, southeast of Cotchford Farm, across from Gills Lap, which makes some cartographical sense: Wrens Warren is also southeast of Pooh's House on Shepard's map of the Hundred Acre Wood. It also makes psychological sense: Wrens Warren can have a creepy sense of place, with trees mangled since the devastating hurricane of 1987. It is especially somber here in winter. A walk on a winter day is an exposed journey into cold, grey austerity: clouds crowd the view toward the picturesque South Downs, and the winds can blow even an optimist's good cheer clear to Scotland. It can be a depressing landscape to a person expecting the scenic and pretty. It can make an Eeyore out of anyone—even those who regard themselves as a Piglet, Pooh, or Tigger at heart.

However, Milne's son Christopher Robin wasn't entirely convinced that "Eeyore's Gloomy Place" was situated anywhere physical. Of all places in the Hundred Acre Wood, this one has a strong psychological dimension. As a boy, the real Christopher Robin gave shape to Eeyore's form with slouched shoulders and downcast head by holding and carrying him this way and that. Milne may have taken this as an opportunity to convey, through a character, his own overcast inner life. It was a part of himself that he kept hidden, his son surmised. Christopher Robin felt "Eeyore's Gloomy Place" was a contained part of his father's heart and mind. Milne was imaginative and expressive—on paper. He was also logical and contained: feelings he kept buttoned inside himself emerged through his characters. And when they did come out, he dressed them up. In *The Enchanted Places*, Christopher Robin says:

> Most of us have small, sad places somewhere in our
> hearts and my father was no exception. Sometimes we let
> our feelings escape in bursts of anger. Sometimes we make
> long, dismal faces. My father did neither. He felt deeply
> but he kept his feelings to himself. Or rather, being a
> writer, he let them escape in his writing. But even here he
> disguised them, unable even in fiction to allow himself to
> take himself too seriously. And so sadnesses as there were
> put on cap and bells and emerged as Eeyore, the old grey
> donkey. Eeyore is gloomy, but you can't feel sorry for him.

It is one thing to understand Eeyore's Gloomy Place as fictional or as a state of mind. It is another thing to walk from the house to the river at Cotchford Farm to encounter incarnations of Eeyore and not wonder about this dimension of Milne's own character.

Donkeys in the pasture
at Cotchford Farm

This happened to me in the meadow where Jessica the donkey was pastured nearly a century ago. Of course, I expected to encounter wild rabbits and maybe even an owl or two during my research for the book. Here, where Jessica was really kept, two real-life, cuddly, walking and braying donkeys approached me. Neither was moody, obstinate, or downcast. In fact, they were curious and sweet and I wanted to tuck them into my pocket or carry them around like stuffed animals.

If it is hard to leave Cotchford Farm, you feel as Milne did: embraced by the place. Cradled between hill, river, and woods, this story-book refuge has things to say about Milne, his family, and the Hundred Acre Wood. Like holding a seashell to ear, we can imagine the

rise and fall of voices by the stream where father and son played cricket. We sense Daphne's presence in the garden when her namesake blooms in winter. A statue of Christopher Robin is set within a flower border, his back to the front door. And a little farther south, Enchanted Forest characters form a carousel around the base of a sundial. All are artifacts of one family's notable literary life in this place. All have been well-preserved by successive residents of Cotchford Farm, including Brian Jones, founder of the Rolling Stones, who lived and died here. Cotchford Farm was the inspiring, cozy place where A. A. Milne wrote and walked and lived for more than thirty years, but there is much more to explore in the forest and woods surrounding it. Grab your boots and knapsack. Let's go there now.

Moody Wrens Warren Valley in autumn

This way, please, to Poohsticks.

Poohsticks Bridge

One day in the Enchanted Forest, Pooh is on a leisurely walk while lost in his own thoughts. It is an aimless pursuit, a journey of random inspiration. As he toddles along, he picks up fir-cones scattered about the forest floor. He is inspired to sing and make up pieces of poetry about them. The result is funny and nonsensical, his head full of fluff: "Here is a myst'ry/About a little fir-tree/Owl says it's *his* tree/And Kanga says it's *her tree*." He arrives at a bridge over a stream, a place where he and Christopher Robin, Piglet, and Roo come to watch the changing river move beneath them. Many of us may be familiar with the scene:

There was a broad track, almost as broad as a road, leading from the Outland to the forest but before it could come to the Forest, it had to cross this river. So, where it crossed, there was a wooden bridge, almost as broad as a road, with wooden rails on each side of it. Christopher Robin could just get his chin on to the top rail, if he wanted to, but it was more fun to stand on the bottom rail, so that he could lean right over, and watch the river slipping slowly beneath him. Pooh could get his chin on to the bottom rail if he wanted to, but it was more fun to lie down and get his head under it, and watch the river slipping slowly away beneath him.

On this particular occasion, though, with his head in poetry and unaware of his footing, Pooh trips just as he comes to the bridge. The fir-cone pops from his paw and lands in the stream. "Bother," he says as it floats slowly under the bridge. But the water is beautiful and interesting and he thinks he would like to watch the river flow as the day is a peaceful one in the forest. He lies down on the wooden bridge and watches the water floating slowly beneath him. It moves less like an excitable brook with a childlike sensibility and more like a river with a growing sense of purpose and direction.

The fir-cone then reappears in a place it wasn't dropped. "That's funny," says Pooh. "I dropped it on the other side," says Pooh, "and it came out on this side! I wonder if it would do it again?" He scampers into the woods to forage for more fir-cones, dropping two at a time into the river and leaning over the bridge to see which one comes out first. He is amazed that the river performs such feats. He does it again and again and again, and by the time he goes home for tea, he has won thirty-six and lost twenty-eight! Such novelty! Pooh invites his friends to join in his new game. They play with sticks instead of fir-cones because sticks are easier to identify.

When Rabbit says "Go!" from "In Which Pooh Invents a New Game and Eeyore Joins In" (*The House at Pooh Corner*)

There is more to the story than founding the game. A sub-plot takes place within the game of Poohsticks. Sometime later on, Pooh, Piglet, and Roo are playing a round of Poohsticks in the river at the edge of the forest. It starts out like any other game, but morphs into one of mystery, drama, suspense—even a little suspicion.

It goes like this: Pooh and his friends are at the edge of the bridge, their sticks at the ready. Rabbit says "Go!" They drop them into the water. They hurry to the other side of the bridge. They lean over the edge in excitement to see whose stick comes out first. Nobody's sticks are yet coming out. Roo's stick is grey and he is excited, as is Piglet. But something strange is floating in the water. It is large and grey and spinning in an eddy. It is a stick, they think. No, it is an Eeyore and he is floating, calm and dignified, swirling around and around with his legs in the air. The friends gasp and exclaim. Eeyore explains that someone has "hooshed" or "nudged" or "bounced" or "boffed" him into the water.

The wooded walk to
Poohsticks Bridge

Who would do that?

Rabbit makes an inquest when Tigger bounds onto the scene. "I didn't really. I had a cough, and I happened to be behind Eeyore, and I said 'Grrr-oppp-ptschschz.'" None of the friends can decide who is to blame or what to do. However, Christopher Robin comes down from the forest to the bridge and they ask *him* what he thinks they should do.

"I think we all ought to play Poohsticks."

So they do. And Eeyore, who has never played before, wins more times than anyone else. Roo falls in twice—the first time by accident and the second time on purpose, because he suddenly sees Kanga coming from the forest and he knows he'll have to go to bed anyhow. So then Rabbit says he'll go with them. Tigger and Eeyore go off together, because Eeyore wants to tell Tigger How to Win at Poohsticks, which you do by letting your stick drop in a twitchy sort of way, if you understand what I mean, Tigger.

OVERLEAF
Poohsticks Bridge

Leaving Cotchford Farm with their backs to Jib Jacks Hill, father and son walked down the dirt lane which today is still as cratered as the moon as it was during Milne's day. They would wander down the dirt path under the canopy of trees to Posingford Wood, which is about half a mile wide and extends from the river at the bottom of a hill to the top of Ashdown Forest. Christopher Robin remembers it as "a gay and friendly wood, the sort of wood you could happily walk through at night, feeling yourself a skillful rather than a brave explorer." It was filled with hazels, willows, sweet chestnuts, and occasional oaks and pines. Medieval farms line the lane, which comes to a serene intersection ancient beyond memory or record. Here a narrower track branches off and begins a gentle descent along the woodland that is filled year-round with liquid warbles and hard cackles of song thrushes, magpies, blue tits, robins, and many more birds of the area.

From *"In Which Pooh Invents a New Game and Eeyore Joins In"* (*The House at Pooh Corner*)

From *"In Which* We Are Introduced to Winnie-the-Pooh and Some Bees, and the Stories Begin" (*Winnie-the-Pooh*)

The Bee Tree

The trees in the Hundred Acre Wood are magical and prominent because they mirror the magnificent trees in Ashdown Forest today and yesterday. From tree hollows to long arms offering an embrace, E. H. Shepard's illustrations show the same sensitive attention to detail and unexpected depth of expression that he conveys in the emotional life of characters. As an illustrator who drew from real life, Shepard set out in Ashdown Forest with notebook and pencils in hand and sketched oaks, beech, walnuts, chestnuts, hazels, and pines as they stood alone, in spinneys, and in woods. They are represented as more than tree homes and places to climb. Stout oaks, arching beech, and solitary pines: these trees have different personalities. They seem to offer not only refuge and shelter, but friendship, too, as interpreted by the different shapes they take. Some say, "Climb me!" while others demurely say, "Sit here."

Ashdown Forest rangers regard birch and other trees as weeds in a garden, given that the forest is intended as a heathland. Trees are not deliberately planted, except in tree clumps, and probably more are removed than grow each year. Single pines are scattered on the open common and look much like those we see throughout the Hundred Acre Wood as well as in the first chapter of *Winnie-the-Pooh*. In those opening pages, we are introduced to Winnie and his love of buzzing bees, which indicates honey is near. "One day when he was out walking, he came to an open place in the middle of the forest, and in the middle of this place was a large oak-tree, and, from the top of the tree, there came a loud buzzing sound."

Ouch! The hazards of honey, from *"In Which* We Are Introduced to Winnie-the-Pooh and Some Bees, and the Stories Begin" (*Winnie-the-Pooh*)

You can never tell with bees.

—Winnie-the-Pooh, from *"In Which* We Are Introduced to Winnie-the-Pooh and Some Bees, and the Stories Begin," *Winnie-the-Pooh*

With the allure of honey, that tree was clearly saying "Climb me!" to Winnie-the-Pooh. And of course, he does just that: he lumbers up the tree, a branch cracks, and the hungry, fluffy bear tumbles branch to branch, down the tree into prickly yellow gorse bush. Ouch!

He composes himself and decides to disguise his body in mud so as to appear like a small black cloud in a blue sky. He asks Christopher Robin for a blue balloon and blows it up. Christopher Robin lets go of him, and, holding onto the string, Pooh floats into the sky, hovering at eye level with the now definitely suspicious bees.

Finally, Pooh decides Christopher Robin must shoot down the balloon with his gun or else he could hover in that state for a very long time. The balloon is gently deflated with a shot, and Pooh comes back down to earth.

Where is this Bee Tree, you may ask? It is everywhere and it is nowhere.

It is one of those places now only alive in the stories of the Hundred Acre Wood. Milne refers to it as an oak tree, and Shepard draws it—for purposes of a bear in search of honey—not round nor full like an oak but more like a columnar beech. No matter, the tree is not any particular place that is now known. Perhaps it was a particular tree at one point, but no longer. Does it matter? Perhaps when you're in the forest with your children, or even by yourself, make finding the bee tree a game. Look everywhere on your walks in Ashdown Forest and the Five Hundred Acre Wood to try to find the one Pooh might have climbed. Listen, too, for the sound of buzzing.

Inspiration for a bee tree, a
Scots pine in Ashdown Forest

The House at Pooh Corner

> The more it snows
> (Tiddely pom),
> The more it goes
> (Tiddely pom),
> The more it goes
> (Tiddely pom),
> On snowing.
> And nobody knows
> (Tiddely pom),
> How cold my toes
> (Tiddely pom),
> How cold my toes
> (Tiddely pom),
> Are growing.
>
> —WINNIE-THE-POOH

It is a wintry scene in chapter one of *The House at Pooh Corner*, Milne's second volume of stories. There is, of course, an adventure to be had. Pooh has created a special Outdoor Song Which Has To Be Sung In The Snow for Eeyore, a friend about whom Pooh has been thinking a lot. He asks Piglet to join him in a walk to Eeyore's house. Empathetic and kind, Pooh wants to sing the song for Eeyore and build a new house for him. Water and weather are often personified by Milne:

> The wind had dropped, and the snow, tired of rushing around in circles trying to catch itself up, now fluttered gently down until it found a place on which to rest, and sometimes the place was Pooh's nose and sometimes it wasn't, and in a little while Piglet was wearing a white muffler round his neck and feeling more snowy behind the ears than he had ever felt before.

Eeyore houses spring up in the woods of Ashdown Forest.

The walk to Eeyore's Gloomy Place becomes colder and colder. They stop near a little pine-wood and sit down on a gate where Pooh thinks they should build Eeyore's new house and call it "Pooh Corner" (because it sounds better than PoohanPiglet corner, Pooh explains). Piglet suggests building the house out of a pile of sticks he has seen on the other side of the wood. They begin fetching the sticks.

Milne loves creating silly misunderstandings. In another part of the Hundred Acre Wood, Eeyore knocks on Christopher Robin's door because he has lost something very important. Eeyore complains about how cold it is, describing the icicles, and says if only others knew how it was on the field, they would feel sorry for him. His house, he tells Christopher Robin, was where he built it in the morning. It was not there in the afternoon. Eeyore and Christopher

Robin walk around the corner of the spinney. In slap-stick comedy dialogue and with good intentions gone awry, Pooh and Piglet have dismantled Eeyore's house—that is, pile of wood—and rebuilt it elsewhere. Oblivious, Eeyore believes the wind has picked it up and moved it. In kindness and modesty, Pooh, Piglet, and

Pooh and Piglet present Eeyore with a "new" house.

Christopher Robin leave him in the wood to enjoy his own clearly superior craftsmanship.

For this story, there is no particular place in Ashdown Forest or the Five Hundred Acre Wood where the house at Pooh Corner took direct inspiration. Inspiration came from many places. Perhaps it

THIS PAGE AND OPPOSITE From *"In Which* a House Is Built at Pooh Corner for Eeyore" (*The House at Pooh Corner*)

From *"In Which* a
House Is Built at Pooh
Corner for Eeyore"
(*The House at Pooh
Corner*)

RIGHT A gate between
Cotchford Farm and
Poohsticks Bridge

Pooh Corner, Hartfield

LEFT **A tea and memorabilia shop in Hartfield**

was the real Christopher Robin's penchant for trees—climbing them, making forts out of them. As he himself said, "If anyone wonders why in the stories so much time seems to be spent in trees or up in trees, the answer is that this, in real life, was how it was." Oak trees, beech trees, maples, pines, and walnut: he enjoyed the bent old trees in an apple orchard down the lane. The house at Pooh Corner could have been inspired by walks in the surroundings; piles of wood can still be seen where Ashdown Forest commoners (owners of particular registered plots of land) collect wood, exercising their right to do so. These days, these little wooden houses which pop up everywhere are sweet reminders of many things: the compassion Pooh and Piglet showed toward their friend and the hours of fun children can have if left alone with a few sticks.

Tiddely pom.

From *"In Which* It Is Shown That Tiggers Don't Climb Trees" (*The House at Pooh Corner*)

Pooh's Thoughtful Spot

Who can say where anybody's thoughtful spot really is? For Pooh, it was in a stream somewhere and nowhere in particular in Ashdown Forest. In the story, *"In Which* It Is Shown That Tiggers Don't Climb Trees,"* this spot is located half-way between Pooh's house and Piglet's house. Sometimes they would meet there when they decided to see each other. It was sheltered from the wind and in full sun, which warmed the rocks and Winnie-the-Pooh's bum. Find a stream where there are rocks worn smooth by water, sit down, listen to the water flow, and there! You have your own Thoughtful Spot.

Gentle streams flow through the real and imaginary forest.

As he was prone to do, Pooh made up a song about it so that people would know what to do here.

> This warm and sunny Spot
> Belongs to Pooh.
> And here he wonders what
> He's going to do.
> Oh, bother, I forgot—
> It's Piglet's too.

The North Pole

At the turn of the twentieth century, expeditions to the North and South Poles were big news, and people had fantastical ideas about the kinds of worlds at the poles. "The theories of the day ranged wildly from a Lost World, to a huge inland sea, to a new civilization, Shangri-La, you name it," explains Bruce Henderson, author of *True North: Peary, Cook, and the Race to the Pole*. Expeditions were front page news. "Everyone seemed to hang on whether the latest expedition had made it, whether the Pole had been reached, and if so, what was up there." This spirit of adventure—rooted in wanderlust, religion, trade, and scientific discovery—led Americans Robert Peary and Frederick Cook to claim, separately, in 1908 and 1909, the discovery of the North Pole (or, at least, the arrival near it, as it was a moving magnetic target). In 1911, to the disappointment of the British who were five weeks behind him, Norwegian Roald Amundsen was the first to arrive at the geographic South Pole.

These expeditions took unbelievable fortitude. A certain type of person was primed for the hardships and courage required for them. It was from a generation of World War I soldiers who survived the Battle of the Somme and other horrors that a rock-hard breed of climbers emerged with a different perspective on life and death. Time on the front left many shaken, questioning what was important. They carried the ethos of the Lost Generation: some were broken, some gritty, some philosophical. Some all three. During the 1920s when Milne became a father and wrote the children's stories, some of these former soldiers were chasing peaks in the name of Britain.

George Mallory and his mountaineering partner Andrew Irvine disappeared on Everest on 8–9 June 1924. The London *Times* published the headline "Mallory and Irvine Killed on Last Attempt" on 21 June 1924. The preparation, climax, and end of these missions would have been the topic at kitchen tables, newspaper agents, and cafés everywhere. Milne would have been interested in discussing current events like this with friends at Garrick Club, one of the

From *"In Which Christopher Robin Leads an Expotition to the North Pole"* (*Winnie-the-Pooh*)

oldest and most highly esteemed private clubs for distinguished men of the day, where he was a member.

This was the big news of the day, and it was in this historical context that Milne wrote the story "*In Which* Christopher Robin Leads an Expotition to the North Pole." It was originally titled "Pooh Discovers the North Pole," which was changed to add mystery about who ends up making the "discovery." As for his other stories, Milne drew on his son's play, his own imagination, and—much like Pooh's house, the Heffalump Trap, Poohsticks Bridge, and elsewhere—a real place in Ashdown Forest.

Perhaps Christopher Robin overheard his father talk about the expeditions to reach the poles as they were unfolding in the 1920s. An introspective boy like Christopher, with parents who cultivated his imaginative play, could have been acting out a small person's version of a larger adventure he had heard about. We can imagine him finding great appeal in such adventures, with a determination to bravely replicate, in his own way, such feats. Either way, it ended up re-imagined in *Winnie-the-Pooh*.

"We are all going on an Expedition," said Christopher Robin, as he got up and brushed himself. "Thank you, Pooh."

"Going on an Expotition?" said Pooh eager. "I don't think I've ever been on one of those. Where are we going to on this Expotition?"

"Expedition, silly old Bear. It's got an 'x' in it."

"Oh!" said Pooh. "I know." But he didn't really.

"We're going to discover the North Pole."

"Oh!" said Pooh again. "What is the North Pole?" he asked.

"It's just a thing you discover," said Christopher Robin carelessly, not being quite sure himself.

"Oh! I see," said Pooh. "Are bears any good at discovering it?"

"Of course they are. And Rabbit and Kanga and all of you. It's an Expedition. That's what an Expedition means. A long line of everybody. You'd better tell the others to get read, while I see if my gun's all right. And we must all bring Provisions."

"Bring what?"

"Things to eat."

"Oh!" said Pooh happily. "I thought you said Provisions. I'll go and tell them." And he stumped off.

With the exception of Tigger, who makes his appearance in the second book, *The House at Pooh Corner*, all the characters we know—and extras, including Rabbit's friends and relations—embark on an Expotition. It has all the elements of a fine Milne adventure story for children: humor and hums; slapstick and puns; danger, suspense, and resolution. And tying the adventure together are soft satin ribbons of compassion, friendship, and heroism.

The North Pole, according to the real Christopher Robin, is not far from Cotchford Farm. For a child, it might seem like quite an adventure as it means walking uphill and downhill, through bracken and gorse and woods, and over a stream—so many worlds to explore. It all took place in Wrens Warren, as the grown Christopher Robin reminisced:

> A path from Gill's Lap takes you to the main road. On the other side the Forest falls away to a valley, then rises again beyond to distant trees. At the bottom of this valley runs a little stream. It is only a very little stream, narrow enough to jump across, shallow enough to paddle across, but it twists and rumbles between steep stony banks. It was here that the North Pole was discovered.

Today that little stream is still there and is known as a ghyll—a steep wooded ravine carved out by water. It makes the sweetest burbling noises around smooth round rocks. It is a perfect setting for a child of six to re-imagine as the mighty Amazon River or Mount Everest—or an arctic pole, if he is playing the role of a brave mountaineer like Mallory.

"There's a South Pole," confides the storybook Christopher Robin to his friends, "and I expect there's an East Pole and a West Pole, though people don't like talking about them."

E. H. Shepard's rendering of this ghyll and the ravine is one of the few illustrations that looks less like the actual landscape in Wrens Warren. The picture shows an open and grassy field. The ghyll in Ashdown Forest is more deeply cut into the landscape and shaded by trees. Perhaps when father and son walked here, they wandered upstream to a more open place. The landscape also changes with trees growing and dying. But now, in the place described by the older Christopher Robin, the banks are steep and the stream channel narrow.

Looking across Wrens Warren in the summer to the North Pole

In Milne's story, between Pooh misunderstanding an "ambush" for a "gorse bush," Eeyore wondering if washing up was really necessary every day, and Owl pontificating with impressive words like "Rhododendron" and "Encyclopedia," Roo falls into a pool of water. There is a loud cry from Kanga. Roo is delighted by this rare moment away from his protective mother and squeals, "Look at me swimming!" as he descends from waterfall to waterfall and pool to pool. Everyone is alarmed. Pooh grabs a stick from somewhere in the forest and extends it across the stream. Kanga holds the other end. Roo drifts into it and climbs to safety. During the rescue, Christopher Robin looks at Pooh holding a special something.

> "Pooh," he said, "where did you find that pole?"
> Pooh looked at the pole in his hands.
> "I just found it," he said. "I thought it ought to be useful. I just picked it up."
> "Pooh," said Christopher Robin solemnly, "the Expedition is over. You have found the North Pole!"

From "*In Which* Christopher Robin Leads an
Expotition to the North Pole" (*Winnie-the-Pooh*)

Where a form of the Expotition took place for the real Christopher Robin

TOP The stream where the North Pole was "discovered"

RIGHT An autumn trail of bracken leads to the ghyll that inspired the North Pole Expotition.

Piglet's House

The Piglet lived in a very grand house in the middle of a beech-tree, and the beech-tree was in the middle of the Forest, and the Piglet lived in the middle of the house. Next to his house was a piece of broken board which had "TRESPASSER'S W" written on it. When Christopher Robin asked the Piglet what it mean, he said it was his grandfather's name, and had been in the family for a long time. Christopher Robin said you *couldn't* be called Trespasser's W, and Piglet said yes, you could, because his grandfather was, and it was short for Trespasser's Will, which was short for Trespassers William. And his grandfather had had two names in case he lost one—Trespasser's after an uncle, and William after Trespassers.

Where is Piglet's house? Perhaps at some point, a home for this little animal who tried very hard to be brave was created in a beech by Christopher Robin. Given the broken "Trespassers Will Be Prosecuted" sign, if we are to be realists, we might say this: Piglet's house was likely inspired by a beech where the forest meets private land. This is where these types of signs crop up in the landscape, not in Ashdown Forest itself. Milne would have seen these on his ambles in the forest. For this reason, Piglet's house was probably inspired by a grove of beeches in the Five Hundred Acre Wood which blew down in the war, as Christopher Robin reflects upon in his autobiography, *The Enchanted Places*. It is the same grove that inspired Owl's house, though it was renamed The Chestnuts.

Of the many wonderful things about the trees in these stories, one is the way they reflect the copious magical nooks of the trees in Ashdown Forest. From oaks to beeches to chestnuts, the dark holes and disappearing crevasses at the trees' bases easily take hold of the imaginations of little ones about the size of Piglet himself. They are still there for you to enjoy.

From "*In Which* Pooh and Piglet Go
Hunting and Nearly Catch a Woozle"
(*Winnie-the-Pooh*)

Tree house possibilities

LEFT Piglet's house? Holes in
trees fascinate children, including
Christopher Robin.

The Stepping Stones

Some of Milne's most lyrical and beautiful writing comes when he describes water. It can be playfully swirling around stones or personified as a child enjoying the sunshine. Throughout the stories, in a paragraph here and a paragraph there, his descriptions of water are exquisite: at one time, a little stream dances and moves like an eager, impatient child. When still, in a pool without a current, water is like a dreaming child. Other times, energetic rivulets high in the Hundred Acre Wood flow into a thoughtful and mature river much in the way we move into adulthood and finally settle down. Fascinated by water, Christopher Robin provided much inspiration as he played on the banks of the river at Cotchford Farm. Like a Thoughtful Spot in the fictional forest, the Stepping Stones could have originated anywhere: in a ghyll on the heathland, in woodlands, or nearer to the farm.

In the story about Poohsticks, the storybook Christopher Robin is walking toward Poohsticks Bridge, unaware that both a new game and a conflict are unfolding. A drama unfolds about who hooshed whom into the river, with bouncy Tigger the focus of attention. For a few moments, Milne writes of Christopher Robin: "If he stood on the bottom rail of the bridge, and leant over, and watched the river slipping away beneath him, then he would suddenly know

A stream in the forest

everything that there was to be known, and he would be able to tell Pooh, who wasn't quite sure about it."

In other ways, water is a source for quiet reflection and a metaphor for the passing of time. In *The House at Pooh Corner*, Milne opens chapter six, "*In Which* Pooh Invents a New Game and Eeyore Joins In," with a lovely description of water flowing from a sprite rivulet to a mature river:

> By the time it came to the edge of the Forest the stream had grown up, so that it was almost a river, and, being grown up, it did not run and jump and sparkle along as it used to do when it was younger, but moved more slowly. For it knew now where it was going, and it said to itself, "There is no hurry. We shall get there some day." But all the little streams higher up in the Forest went this way and that, quickly, eagerly, having so much to find out before it was too late.

The stepping stones where Pooh sits are in a stream near heather, in a place reminiscent of Wrens Warren Valley. In the summer when water runs shallow, stones are exposed and beckon children to leap upon them. Milne saw the spirit and mind of a child in the way water moved. We see this tenderness in chapter ten of *Winnie-the-Pooh*, "*In Which* Christopher Robin Gives Pooh a Party, and We Say Good-bye."

> One day when the sun had come back over the Forest, bringing with it the scent of May, and all the streams of the Forest were tinkling happily to find themselves their own pretty shape again, and the little pools lay dreaming of the life they had seen and the big things they had done, and in the warmth and quiet of the Forest the cuckoo was trying over his voice carefully and listening to see if he liked it, and wood-pigeons were complaining gently to themselves in their lazy comfortable way that it was the other fellow's fault, but it didn't matter much.

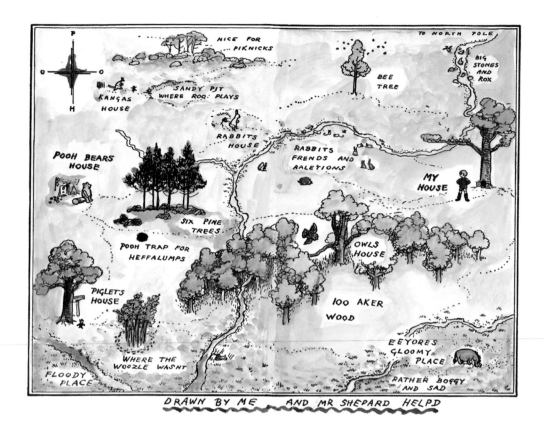

The map labels read:

- TO NORTH POLE
- P (compass top), with compass rose
- NICE FOR PIKNICKS
- BIG STONES AND ROX
- BEE TREE
- SANDY PIT WHERE ROO PLAYS
- KANGAS HOUSE
- RABBITS HOUSE
- RABBITS FRENDS AND RALETIONS
- MY HOUSE
- POOH BEARS HOUSE
- SIX PINE TREES
- OWLS HOUSE
- POOH TRAP FOR HEFFALUMPS
- PIGLETS HOUSE
- 100 AKER WOOD
- EEYORES GLOOMY PLACE
- WHERE THE WOOZLE WASNT
- FLOODY PLACE
- RATHER BOGGY AND SAD
- DRAWN BY ME AND MR SHEPARD HELPD

A Nice Place for Picnics

Have you watched a child tracing his or her finger over trails on the map of the Hundred Acre Wood "Drawn by Me and Mr. Shepard Helpd"? Look to see how children are transported to a different world. There is comfort gazing into the imagined world on the map. It is, as we are told, illustrated by a child (with just a bit of "help" from Mr. Shepard). Being thus, it is a quintessential hide-and-seek landscape, with woods and tree houses providing refuge and places to be small. We instantly feel a part of the landscape: the tall summer grass brushing against our shins as we run in the sun; the cold, clear streams on our feet; the feeling of being a baby bird in a nest as we hide in a tree hollow like Christopher Robin in the walnut tree at Cotchford Farm.

The Baker family—Ian, Alice, and Jill—picnic under an oak tree near Broadstone Heath.

OPPOSITE The Hundred Acre Wood where the adventures took place

If we look at the compass rose on the map, we chuckle to see it doesn't indicate direction, in a north-south-east-west fashion, but direction toward P-O-O-H. Up near the "P" is a place noted as "Nice for Piknicks." As readers of the Winnie-the-Pooh stories, we know that the characters are always on an amble, expedition, or some other adventure, and wherever they want to stop, rest, and eat, they just might. We can imagine Milne and Christopher Robin taking walks and carrying biscuits and drinks in a knapsack. Kids need refreshment to keep going sometimes. There are ample places, we imagine as we trace our fingers over Shepard's map, to stop and rest in this imagined world. It is like that in Ashdown Forest as well as the Hundred Acre Wood: they are one in the same. Throughout Ashdown Forest, there are benches and open space to set down a blanket or rug and enjoy a picnic. Thorny gorse needs to be avoided in the heathland, but the edges of woods are often grassier. Walking on any trails will provide ample opportunity to find a place "Nice for Piknicks." It's about the setting and company: enjoying a breathtaking panorama, fresh air, and nature, and perhaps a few cucumber sandwiches and cocktail sausages.

A bench for tea and a view of the world

The Old Grey Donkey, Eeyore, stood by himself in a thistly corner of the Forest, his front feet well apart his head on one side, and thought about things. Sometimes he thought sadly to himself, "Why?" and sometimes he thought, "Wherefore?" and sometimes he thought, "Inasmuchas which?"—and sometimes he didn't quite know what he *was* thinking about.

—From "*In Which* Eeyore Loses a Tail and Pooh Finds One," *Winnie-the-Pooh*

Owl's House

It is chapter four of *Winnie-the-Pooh*. This is our introduction to Eeyore, Owl, and Pooh's compassion for his friends. In the story, Pooh is on a walk in the Hundred Acre Wood. He stumps up to Eeyore, noticing that there is something wrong with him. We know the story of Eeyore losing his tail: "That Accounts for a Good Deal," Eeyore says. "It Explains Everything. No Wonder." Pooh feels his friend has merely misplaced his tail, while Eeyore thinks someone has taken it. To deal with it, Pooh sets out in the Hundred Acre Wood to consult with Owl, as he knows the "Crustimoney Proseed-cake"—that is, customary procedures—for dealing with such matters. Milne draws a beautiful picture of the landscape through which Pooh walks.

> It was a fine spring morning in the Forest as he started out. Little soft clouds played happily in a blue sky, skipping from time to time in front of the sun as if they had come to put it out, and then sliding away suddenly so that the next might have his turn. Through them and between them the sun shone bravely; and a copse which had worn its firs all the year round seemed old and dowdy now beside the green lace which the beeches had put on so prettily. Through copse and spinney marched Bear; down open slopes of gorse and heather, over rocky beds of streams, up steep bands of sandstone into the heather again; and so at least, tired and hungry, to the Hundred Acre Wood. For it was in the Hundred Acre Wood that Owl lived.

From "*In Which* Eeyore Loses a Tail and
Pooh Finds One" (*Winnie-the-Pooh*)

A grand chestnut tree

Owl lives at Chestnuts, "an old-world residence of great charm, which was grander than anybody else's, or seemed so to Bear, because it had both a knocker and a bell-pull." Underneath this knocker is a notice: "PLES RING IF AN RNSER IS REQIRD." And below the bell-pull there is another notice, which says: "PLZ CNOKE IF AN RNSR IS NOT REQID."

Though Milne placed Chestnuts in a landscape reminiscent of Ashdown Forest, Owl's house was really based on an ancient beech tree, one of about half a dozen, in what the real Christopher Robin remembers as the "dark and mysterious" Five Hundred Acre Wood, a place very different from the open expanse of Ashdown's heather and gorse. "It looked as if over the centuries it had grown tired of holding up its arms to the sky and had allowed its lower branches to droop." One branch in particular stretched out horizontally and then bowed downwards to the ground. As a boy, Christopher Robin would sit on it. Sometimes he would walk along it and leap off it into a pile of leaves on the ground. He could balance and jump and wiggle along the moss-covered branches toward the trunk as far as he dared. He remembers the four of them—his mother, father, himself, and Nanny—visiting this grand tree and in later years recalling that his father saw the tree in a new way, as writers can sometimes do with their imaginations:

> Of those who watched, one perhaps to dream, to see the branch snaking to the ground and someone walking up it, walking easily, walking all the way, up the steep bit, right up to the trunk, finding there a door with a knocker and a bell, a door in the tree and someone living behind it. Who? Who? Could it be an owl? Could it be Owl that the visitor had come to see?

Standing on such an elegant branch, Pooh realizes the bell-rope looks familiar. He has seen it before. He tells Owl, who said he picked it off a bush, that someone he knows is quite attached to it. Pooh takes it to Eeyore, and Christopher Robin nails it back in its rightful place. In this imaginary world, Owl's House is the center of the Hundred Acre Wood. But the tree itself was real—a majestic beech in the Five Hundred Acre Wood where the real Christopher Robin played. That particular beech grove vanished during World War II, but there are new beeches that grow in the same area now.

Leaves of a sweet chestnut tree (*Castanea sativa*) in the Five Hundred Acre Wood

LEFT Ashdown Forest Ranger Mike Yates with a majestic 200-year-old beech

The Sandy Pit Where Roo Plays

One day, Kanga and Baby Roo show up in the forest. It is unexpected. This method of carrying a little one in a pocket is strange and unknown to the animals. Perplexed by the newcomer, Pooh consults with Rabbit, who loves order, methodologies, and bureaucracy. To preserve the status quo, Rabbit, who also likes to be busy, takes out a pencil, licks the tip, and hatches a harebrained plan to snatch Baby Roo from Kanga when she is not looking. Rabbit, Piglet, and Pooh think this will somehow entice her to leave the forest. When she wonders what has happened, they can then say *"Aha!"* Of course, they have no plan whatsoever for after "Aha!"

One quiet afternoon, the three find Roo playing in the Sandy Pit on top of Galleons Lap. On the map of the Hundred Acre Wood, it is not far from Rabbit's House and Kanga's House. Roo is practicing how to be a kangaroo, with little leaps in the soft sand where, if he falls, he has a nice place to land. He spends a lot of time falling into mouse holes. The trio somehow manages to distract Kanga, pop Piglet into her pocket, and off she hops. Rabbit takes Roo home and immediately grows fond of him—which is not according to plan. Pooh then loses track of the mission and jumps about the sandy place pretending to be Kanga.

By the time Kanga has unbuttoned her pocket at home and realizes a joke has been played on her, she decides to go along: Piglet gets a firm scrubbing in the bath and a spoonful of extract of malt despite his loud, repeated protestations that he is Piglet, not Roo. Naturally, the magnanimous Christopher Robin appears on the scene and resolves the problem. In the end, in typical Milne conciliation and harmony, great friendships have been established in the Hundred Acre Wood: Roo spends every Tuesday with his great new friend Rabbit, Kanga teaches Pooh how to jump, and Piglet spends more time with Christopher Robin. Perhaps Milne's gentle lesson is to get to know those who are different from us.

From "*In Which* Kanga and Baby Roo Come to the
Forest, and Piglet Has a Bath" (*Winnie-the-Pooh*)

Roo's sandy pit

LEFT White sandy
path atop Gills Lap

LEFT White sandy
path atop Gills Lap

In Ashdown Forest, there is a real Sandy Pit that inspired this story. A short walk north on a sandy track from the Gills Lap tree clump, it is a low and wide depression, the remnants of a former quarry for stone used in area roads. Walking up here from Cotchford Farm, the Milnes would have passed it on their way to panoramic views atop this heathland. There are many such depressions throughout Ashdown Forest. This one is less a sandy pit than a place where wetland plants now grow. It is surrounded in part by Scots pines and makes a delightful place for children to practice bouncing like a kangaroo.

Rabbit's House

In the second chapter of *Winnie-the-Pooh*, we see Pooh walking through the Enchanted Forest, humming to himself. He had earlier composed a little hum while doing his Stoutness Exercises in front of a mirror. *Tra-la-la, tra-la-la, Rum-tum-tiddle-um-tum*. It is a beautiful sunny day to be humming. With his hands behind his back, Pooh saunters through the dry golden grass of the forest, looking up at birds in the sky and enjoying the new day. Pooh is humming this hum to himself, wondering what the others in the forest are doing, when he comes to a hole in a sandy bank.

> "Aha!" said Pooh. (*Rum-tum-tiddle-um-tum.*) "If I know anything about anything, that hole means Rabbit," he said, "and Rabbit means Company," he said, "and Company means Food and Listening-to-Me-Humming and such like. *Rum-tum-tum-tiddle-um.*"

He pops his head into the hole and wonders aloud if anybody is home. Sudden scuffling noises come from within—surprised rabbits are wont to be jumpy—and then there is an awkward silence. Pooh thinks and calls again. "Bother!" says Pooh. "Isn't there anybody here at all?"

"Nobody," a voice calls. Pooh tries again.

Using different voices, Rabbit denies that he is really in. Finally Pooh is able to verify that he is indeed Pooh and receives an invitation to enter Rabbit's home in the ground. Pushing his tubby girth through the hole in the bank, he just squeezes through into Rabbit's house. It is a cozy country home with a cupboard painted green, canisters on shelves, and a table where Rabbit sets out mugs and plates for Elevenses, a mid-morning snack. Rabbit offers bread with condensed milk or honey. Pooh just takes both. As we well know, when it is time to leave, Pooh becomes a Wedged Bear in Great Tightness. In other words, stuck.

Pillow mounds

Whenever the animals find themselves in conflicts, they fetch Christopher Robin from the other end of the forest. He is revered because he can read. He is a calm and loving problem solver. "There is only one thing to be done," he surmises. "We shall have to wait for you to get thin again." Rabbit, practical though lacking tact on occasion, wonders if, in this instance, he might use Pooh's back legs as a towel-horse.

Throughout the forest and woods where Milne and his family explored, signs of wildlife abound—foxes, rabbits, stoats, weasels, squirrels, shrews, mice, and badgers. There are small holes and there are bigger burrows. A child of four or five who bends down to look into a rabbit hole might conjure a whole world of domesticity

Examples of pillow
mounds in Dartmoor
National Park

inside the den. It makes a great activity on walks with children to
stop and guess what kind of animal lives in a particular hole in the
ground, and whether it is a den, set, warren, burrow, or hill. Rabbit's
home was inspired by rich rabbit history in Ashdown Forest.

What makes Ashdown Forest unique is its late medieval pillow
mounds, or artificial rabbit warrens. They are so named on account
of their shape. These low stone mounds, which are about thirty to
sixty feet long and twenty feet wide, were once covered with earth,
enclosed, and used as artificial rabbit warrens. Remnants of these
curious earthworks dot the British countryside and are seen
throughout Ashdown Forest. Much of the enclosed land here was
historically used for intensive rabbit farming. It explains why the

name "warren" is included in so many of the historic names of the area, including Broadstone Warren, Hindleap Warren, Press Ridge Warren, and Crowborough Warren.

It may seem strange now to imagine that rabbits were once regarded as valuable, as they are such a common sight, peeking from under gorse, scampering through the heather, and becoming icons of children's literature through Beatrix Potter's *The Tales of Peter Rabbit*. But rabbits are not native to England. They were an important source of protein before sheep grazing, but how they got to Ashdown Forest and England has been a source of debate until recently. Academics questioned whether rabbits were introduced by the Normans or the Romans. It was thought the Normans introduced them to Britain in the eleventh or twelfth century for their fur and meat, as there is no Old English word for rabbit. It is possible that rabbits died out after the Romans left (albeit inconceivable, given the rabbit's reproduction rate and penchant for escape).

However, the debate over the origins of rabbits in Britain was resolved in 2005 when 2,000-year-old rabbit remains were uncovered in an archaeological dig in Norfolk. Pottery next to the butchered rabbit remains were dated to the second century AD, substantiating what ancient Roman writer and scholar Marcus Terrentius Varro (116–27 BC) had written about legions bringing rabbits with them from Spain, where they had been served as an epicurean delight. While pillow mounds in Ashdown Forest are thought to be from medieval times, it was not the Normans who introduced them. Rabbit was an excellent form of income especially in rural areas where there was sandy heathland which was poor for crops but excellent for burrowing. Rabbit warrens or farms were carefully tended here, and warreners, special officials who looked after the rabbits for the Lord of the Manor, simply needed to toss a mature male and female rabbit into the enclosed warren with enough grass, and a profit could be turned.

These days, pillow mounds in Ashdown Forest may be difficult to identify. They may appear to be soft crinkles or natural undulations in the landscape. Keep a lookout on your walks. Close to Cotchford Farm, one extends north from the tree clump King's Standing, a couple of miles south of Gills Lap and the Enchanted Place tree clumps. It can be seen as you approach from the car park, extending from the cluster of Scots pines northward, suggesting the trees were planted over the old warren.

During the week in which Pooh is actively slimmed, Christopher Robin takes it upon himself to read to the North end of Pooh while Rabbit hangs his washing on the South end. When the week of rationing comes to an end, Rabbit and all of his friends-and-relations grab a hold of one another and pull and pull and—*Ow!* and *Oh!* and out he pops like a cork from a bottle—Pooh is free from the rabbit hole. Christopher Robin, Rabbit, and all of his friends-and-relations tumble head-over-heels backward, with Pooh landing on top of them all. Pooh stands up, and, with equanimity and gratitude, nods a thank you to his friends and carries on with his walk of a week earlier, Christopher Robin looking after him and saying, "Silly old Bear!"

Galleons Lap

If there is a central landscape to all the Winnie-the-Pooh stories, it would be Gills Lap (pronounced like "Jill"), or Galleons Lap as Milne renamed it. It is here that many stories—both real and fictional—originate. Galleons Lap is the luminescent background we see peeking through the trees of the Enchanted Place, the place where Christopher Robin realizes it is time to separate from his toys. On paper and in reality, the world seems entirely open. It is a large, sandy plateau with views to Wrens Warren, to the South Downs, and beyond. There are paths and tracks, heather and gorse, bracken and grasses. Solitary pines and tree clumps can be seen for miles around. The wind is bracing. The sky is big.

To this day, Gills Lap is just as E. H. Shepard drew it. Milne brought Shepard here with his notepads and pencils so that he could draw Ashdown Forest from real life. It is where the Milnes

OVERLEAF
Galleons Lap is based on the real Gills Lap.

Gorse

walked together as well as alone through the years, the place Christopher Robin could see from his nursery windows at Cotchford Farm. Many years later, the grown Christopher Robin wrote, Gills Lap "is exactly as described, an enchanted spot before Pooh ever came along to add to its magic." The memorial for Milne and Shepard is here as well. Deliberately unmarked, it encourages people to take a walk of discovery, as Milne would have liked.

The Enchanted Place

In the final chapter of *The House at Pooh Corner*, there is a sense even among the smallest animals of the Enchanted Forest that "Things were going to be Different." Christopher Robin is going away, but nobody in the forest knows why. Rabbit decides he must figure out an official response to the confusion and hopelessness. He calls a meeting where Eeyore is asked to read aloud the written proposal which he has tucked behind his ear. It is called "POEM" and he reads it aloud to the animals gathered on the grass.

> Christopher Robin is going.
> At least I think that he is.
> Where?
> Nobody knows
> But he is going—
> I mean he goes
> (*To rhyme with "knows"*)
> Do we care?
> (*To rhyme with "where"*)
> We do
> Very much.

There is more of "POEM" to read in Milne's story. When Eeyore finishes reading "POEM," he asks for a little clapping, please, and the Rissolution is signed by POOH, WOL, PIGLET, EOR, RABBIT, KANGA, BLOT, and SMUDGE (which is Roo's signature). The motley bunch then head off in the direction of Christopher Robin's tree house to present said Rissolution. The mood in Christopher Robin's tree house is awkward. Nobody says a word. Sadness lingers in the air as the animals sense that change of some sort is afoot. While Christopher Robin reads the Rissolution, everybody slowly slips away like Eeyore has, not knowing why they are doing so themselves. Only Pooh remains. Pooh then says:

"What I like best in the whole world is Me and Piglet going to see You, and You saying, 'What about a little something?' and Me saying, 'Well, I shouldn't mind a little something, should you, Piglet,' and it being a hummy sort of day outside and birds singing."

"I like that too," said Christopher Robin, "but what I like *doing* best is Nothing."

"How do you do Nothing?" asked Pooh, after he had wondered for a long time.

"Well, it's when people call out at you just as you're going off to do it, What are you going to do, Christopher Robin, and you say, Oh, nothing, and then you go and do it."

"Oh, I see," said Pooh.

"This is a nothing sort of thing that we're doing now."

"Oh, I see," said Pooh again.

"It means just going along, listening to all the things that you can't hear, and not bothering."

"Oh!" said Pooh.

While Eeyore famously fusses and Piglet constantly fears, Rabbit evaluates and Owl pontificates, Pooh is a listener and accepts what life brings. He doesn't try too hard. He doesn't fight his honey habit nor growing Buddha tummy. His quirky friends' idiosyncrasies roll off his back.

But there is more than a conversation between a boy and his bear. "Doing Nothing" is a euphemism. Milne is really talking about the space and place a child occupies in his mind before leaving the haven of home for outside challenges. It is the limited time

More than a clump of trees, an Enchanted Place

in life when free time and Doing Nothing is acceptable, a time before a life of schedules and deadlines.

In the story, the imaginary Christopher Robin, wearing red shorts, a simple shirt, and a hat, walks hand in hand with Pooh toward the clump of Scots pines.

> They walked on, thinking of This and That, and by-and-by, they came to an enchanted place on the very top of the Forest called Galleons Lap which is sixty-something trees in a circle; and Christopher Robin knew that it was enchanted because nobody had ever been able to count whether it was sixty-three or sixty-four, not even when he tied a piece of string around each tree after he had counted it. Being enchanted, its floor was not like the floor of the Forest, gorse and bracken and heather, but close-set grass, quiet and smooth and green. It was the only place in the Forest where you could sit down carelessly, without getting up again almost at once and looking for somewhere else. Sitting there they could see the whole world spread out until it reached the sky, and whatever there was all the world over was with them in Galleons Lap.

E. H. Shepard illustrates the Enchanted Place as a beautiful sanctuary of golden light and long thoughtful shadows. It is, in real life, illuminated and wholly enchanting and much more, a place where magical thinking is still allowed. Indeed with a sweep of a stick from the forest floor, Good King Christopher Robin knights Sir Pooh de Bear on the shoulders. Here a child can be king or queen of an imaginary world where wonderful things can happen. And this sort of Doing Nothing is rather important. For children, slow and unstructured time cultivates imagination at an important time in their development. For adults, Doing Nothing is the antidote to Always Doing Something, a reminder to slow down the pace. Life need not be lived at a hectic, breakneck speed. Less rabbit, more bear.

The importance
of imaginary play,
from "*In Which*
Christopher Robin
and Pooh Come to
an Enchanted Place,
and We Leave Them
There" (*The House
at Pooh Corner*)

The Enchanted Place is lovingly recalled by adult readers, as it represents a time and space when they themselves made sense of their world through imaginative play. Written in 1928, four years before the real Christopher Robin goes to school, the story may also have been Milne the father reflecting on the time when his own son would leave home for Stowe, a boarding school in Buckingham-shire. It could also be a mixture of Milne reflecting back on leaving home at eleven for Westminster. Perhaps it was a reflection on childhood itself, or a combination of all three, as life and art blend together.

From "*In Which* Christopher Robin and Pooh Come to an Enchanted
Place, and We Leave Them There" (*The House at Pooh Corner*)

In the story, Christopher Robin is stretched on the grass and contemplative, unsure about the new place he is going. The animals of the forest feel the change, and he does, too. It is, he sadly tells Pooh, a place where he will be busy doing schoolish things.

Christopher Robin asks Pooh to visit this collection of trees when he is away, and to promise never to forget him. It is a poignant scene in children's literature: the child in all of us who must bid farewell to childhood and our stuffed animals. Where Christopher Robin is going, the play toys cannot go: they need to be stored away in an attic trunk or on bedroom shelves.

> "Pooh, *promise* you won't forget about me, ever. Not even when I'm a hundred."
>
> Pooh thought for a little.
>
> "How old will *I* be then?"
>
> "Ninety-nine."
>
> Pooh nodded.

Like Poohsticks Bridge, Galleons Lap, and Roo's Sandy Pit, the Enchanted Place can be aligned with a real spot. More than a famous figurative world in children's fiction, it is a cluster of trees

From *"In Which* Christopher Robin and Pooh Come to an Enchanted Place, and We Leave Them There" (*The House at Pooh Corner*)

in Ashdown Forest, and is officially and conveniently known as the Enchanted Place. It is planted with Scots pine, an evergreen coniferous tree capable of growing taller than a hundred feet. Scots pine was widespread across the British Isles before the Last Glacial Maximum when ice sheets were at their maximum spread. As the climate warmed, it became extinct from most of the British Isles around 5,500 years ago except in Scotland and at Kielder, Northumberland. Now, it is one of the few trees tolerated in a landscape assiduously maintained for its heath. While most of the Scots pines are dotted singly throughout the landscape, the forest contains eight deliberately planted clumps, all of which have historical significance. The Enchanted Place is the one closest to Cotchford Farm and the one most visited by the Milnes on their walks. The other clumps scattered throughout Ashdown Forest are Gills Lap Clump, Friend's Clump, Millennium Clump, Crows Nest Clump, King's Standing, Millbrook Clump, Wych Cross Clump, and Kennedy Clump—this last one planted to celebrate John F. Kennedy's visit to Forest Row on 30 June 1963, just a few months before he was assassinated.

JFK visiting Forest Row

From the car park at Gills lap, there is a flat ridge path to the Enchanted Place clump on the horizon. Walking into the clump feels both charming and dangerous. On the one hand, there is a sense of returning to a place familiar from early memory: like an egg in a nest, the comfort of sitting in the lap of someone who read aloud stories when we were young. Even if we have never been there before, the Enchanted Place is already known to us, a mix of warm early memories and a place already constructed in our mind's eye. The pleasure is doubled, tripled, and quadrupled when we visit the actual Enchanted Place. For a few moments, we may feel a fleeting return to childhood as our youngsters build Eeyore homes among the pines, count if there are sixty-three or sixty-four trees, and run in and out of clumps, from light to dark and dark to light.

OVERLEAF **Kings Standing with extending pillow mounds**

These trees, both in real life and in Shepard's drawings, bring us happiness on many levels. Christopher Robin and Pooh step up into the cluster as light streams in from the east or the west. The sky glows. Bark glistens. The grass is newly green. It is childhood, the spring of our lives. The drawings are so emotive, so tender, and so iconic that it may be hard to separate them from the real place. But why bother? Why separate memory from what we see? The fusion of fiction and nonfiction, the real and the fantasy worlds, the links between literature and landscape, are so joyful. And it is there in Ashdown Forest where we perceive the Enchanted Place through the prism of many: through Milne, Shepard, the fictional Christopher Robin, the real Christopher Robin, our children, our own childhood memories, and our adult experiences. There in the real Enchanted Place, the dense canopy of Scots pines prevents much overhead light from entering. This creates a soft carpet of blue-tinged pine needles free of the surrounding bracken, yellow gorse, and heather. It is, as Milne noted, one of the few places in the forest where it's possible to comfortably sit without worrying about being pricked by gorse or poked by heather.

Long shadows cast by Scots pines near Kanga's sandy pit—so beautifully captured by Shepard in the Enchanted Place

In any season, the Enchanted Place serves as a refuge. In winter, when wind and rain drive hard on the heathland, one can step inside the Enchanted Place to find shelter. Sit down. Lean against the trunk of a pine. Listen to the wind in the tree tops. In the summer, enjoy the respite of this shady grove. Bring a copy of *The House at Pooh Corner* and read it aloud or to yourself. No one will think you strange. Build an Eeyore house and crawl inside.

The Milne family and Nanny often took walks here—"the four of us in single file threading the narrow paths that run through the heather," Christopher Robin recalled. From his nursery window at Cotchford Farm, which lies in a valley, he could look up the steadily

An Eeyore house
inside the Enchanted
Place in winter

RIGHT Inside the
ordered Gills Lap
tree clump near the
car park

rising land of gorse and bracken and see Gills Lap. There on top was a clump of pines. It is exactly as Milne described it and Shepard drew it, Christopher Robin noted.

The Enchanted Place is among the most memorable settings in children's literature. It sits atop the highest point in Ashdown Forest, a shady gathering of trees seen for miles around. Both meeting place and metaphor, it is where a boy asks his bear to remember him as he leaves childhood behind. Clusters of trees strikes deep chords in us for protection and refuge just as friendships do for children, their stuffed animals, and adults.

Here in the very last Winnie-the-Pooh story, one with the most revisions and edits in Milne's original manuscript, are some of the most famous last words written for children when Christopher Robin and Pooh go off together: "But wherever they go, and whatever happens to them on the way," Milne writes, "in that enchanted place on top of the Forest, a little boy and his Bear will always be playing."

A Visitor's Guide

The FLORA and FAUNA of ASHDOWN FOREST

Pooh's Forest and Ashdown Forest are identical.

—Christopher Robin Milne, *The Enchanted Places*

Milne's stories captivate us as children and resonate with us well into adulthood. No matter the years that pass between two and thirty-two—between the time we are read our first *Winnie-the-Pooh*, to the time we first visit Ashdown Forest as parents, our two-year-olds on our shoulders—we all remember our snuggly teddy bears and the magical landscapes of our own childhood. Whether we tromped in sun-dappled rural fields or in weedy city lots, we had those treasured companions in tow—our first friends, our playmates, our soul mates.

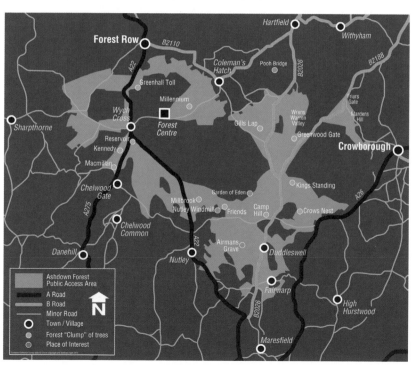

Wrens Warren Valley, Ashdown Forest in late summer

LEFT **Map of Ashdown Forest, East Sussex**

Though the Hundred Acre Wood is a product of Milne's fertile imagination, the real Ashdown Forest awaits you. Here, the real and the imaginary landscapes coalesce into novelty and nostalgia. Over a year of research, I explored the forest on foot—hiking through heather, hopping over rocks in streams, listening to birds and bees, and attempting to climb a pine tree or two (resulting in prickly gorse in the bum). I also know the fabled setting of the Hundred Acre Wood so well that I can recite the stories in my sleep, laughing still at Milne's wit and warmth. As I became utterly immersed in the history of Milne, Shepard, and all things Pooh, the magic of the Hundred Acre Wood has never waned. (With the exception of a wet and blustery day in February, when I "tested" whether the Enchanted Place was really so enchanted. Alas, the answer is that it is not. A pint of Harveys ale in front of a pub fire may be more enchanting.)

Though the Hundred Acre Wood is imaginary, you can still see it in the gorse, heather, and Scots pines of Ashdown Forest, which lives on and changes slowly over time. Milne's classic stories also live on, showing no signs of abating in the hearts and minds of readers around the world. What many are not aware of, however, is how much history is present in this ancient landscape, shaped as it was (and is) by kings, commoners, and conservators. The forest has a story of its own—one that began long before Milne's characters ambled in and became a part of it.

As visitors to the forest, we too can become part of the story. Milne would be happy to know that children were enjoying the outdoors, exploring and ambling in Ashdown Forest much like Winnie-the-Pooh and friends did on their gentle adventures. The best way to explore the forest is to follow in Milne's footsteps and take a stroll. A lifelong joy and habit for the author, walking sets the mind adrift, clarifying and organizes thoughts—a vital process for writers. Walking allows a pace for discovering small, new things: how gorse has the faint smell of coconut in spring, that the red dragonflies hovering over bogs are actually rare, and that the

Tranquil travels
by foot

nocturnal bird calls are from the threatened nightjar. Across the forest, paths and trails crisscross over ten square miles, offering many walking opportunities. To paraphrase Milne, don't just stay in your corner of the forest. Venture in and discover new plants and animals, and see what makes this landscape so special and highly protected. And if you have a sneaking suspicion that Pooh and Piglet might appear around a gorse bush or that Tigger might be up in a tree, you can be forgiven for confusing the real and the imagined. It's easy to do so in this storybook landscape.

Visitors to Ashdown Forest may want to negotiate with a map. The first one to pop to mind may be Shepard's hand-drawn "Hundred Acre Wood," with tree houses, rivers, and woods. I am often

Winnie the Pooh, Ashdown Forest background 1926 (where it all happened) a sketch made on the spot when I visited it with A. A. Milne

Shepard's handwritten caption reads, "Winnie the Pooh, Ashdown Forest background 1926 (where it all happened) a sketch made on the spot when I visited it with A. A. Milne."

asked if these two places are one in the same. *Can Shepard's map be used as a guide to Ashdown Forest?* Of course, we can define our visits any way we like, but for those curious about the forest's natural history, the Shepard map may be gently tucked it into your rucksack. It is indeed imaginary and—charmingly so—a hodgepodge of places that Milne and Shepard created for a child's imagination.

For a more realistic map, the Ashdown Forest Centre is a great starting point. Brochures, which can be picked up on location or downloaded from the Forest Centre website, contain walks and information highlighting the archaeology, military history, and environmental history of the forest. Most walks are under two miles, but they can be combined for longer ambles.

An Unfamiliar Forest

Most Pooh pilgrims start their explorations in the woodland where
Poohsticks Bridge is located or atop the heather on Gills Lap, where
the whole world gloriously spreads out from the South Downs
nearly up to London. Among the first things visitors may wonder,
standing in the open heathland with arms outstretched, is, "How is
this a forest?"

As a visitor, you may find this forest before you perplexing,
since a forest is popularly understood to be a big densely wooded
area. But the word has several ancient meanings as well—an exten-
sive land tract; an area set aside for hunting by royalty and others
and subject to special laws; a wild, uncultivated waste—and Ashdown Forest has been all those things. From Mesolithic hunters to
Roman soldiers, coppice workers to Anglo-Saxon drovers, kings
to commoners to conservators, people have long used the land,

sculpting it into the forest we see today. It is full of history, rare in habitat, and rich in paradox. It is both deceiving and enchanting—a place where forest rangers protect and conserve flora and fauna while actively removing trees as if they were weeds in a garden. When you see the hills of heather and bracken, woods and streams, it looks wild and natural—but it is not. It is a man-made landscape, shaped by hunting, grazing, the collection of wood and bracken by commoners, iron manufacturing, and military training. At times in its past, this forest has been vilified as a wasteland, while today it is coveted as a rare lowland of heath with international importance and protection. When Winnie-the-Pooh and his friends ambled onto the scene, they added another dimension to its rich sense of place—a beloved literary one. For the best view of the forest and surrounding countryside, head first to Gills Lap, one of the tallest points in the forest and a plateau. Here, you will find a landscape straight from Shepard's drawings, with magnificent views, tree clumps, and sandy heathland.

Origins of a Name

If you are of a botanical bent, you may, not surprisingly, search for ash trees on your first visit to Ashdown Forest. The name is paradoxical until you remember that the British Isles have a rich toponymy—the study of place names—from its linguistic, political, and settlement histories. Old and modern English, Scottish and Irish Gaelic, and Welsh are often seen in geographical place names. A drive from Cornwall in the south to the Hebrides in the north will take you through landscapes with roots in diverse other cultures and language including Anglo-Norman, Anglo-Saxon, Roman, and Viking.

Nobody is quite certain how the forest came to be called Ashdown. Given the name, visitors may come expecting to find ash trees, and then become perplexed to find them absent. The soil conditions in this area are not favorable for ash. But the history of the forest's name suggests other possibilities. The 1929 English

Place-Name Society's *Volume VI, the Place-Names of Sussex* lists the earliest written names of Ashdown from 1200 to 1340 as Hessedon, Ashendon, Assedune, Aysshedone, and Ashedoune. These early forms of "ash" suggest that the first part of the name—*aescen*—is an adjective used to describe a *dún*, an Old English word for a down or hill. Was it a hill overgrown with ash trees? Historians think this was probably not the case unless a dún took its name from a prominent ash tree which may have grown somewhere here. The more likely scenario is that a dún took its name from an individual or people named Aesc or Aesca, hence Aesca's dún—Ashdown—or, the hill of Aesca.

The Ancient Rights of Commoners

Ashdown Forest is distinctive from its surroundings in part because of the way people used the land and its resources for over nine hundred years. Soon after arriving in England in 1066, William the Conqueror set aside this forest for deer hunting. A keen huntsman who imported highly-stylized French hunting rituals to England, he gave the area, which extended from Lewes to the west to Hasting in the East, to his half-brother Robert, Count of Mortain. It came with the strict proviso that the king, along with his sons and noble friends, was able to keep deer here and hunt when he pleased.

Fallow deer

Red deer stag

But there were other people on the land as well: a group of ordinary people who were, like the "common man," not part of the priesthood or nobility. As such, they were called commoners. There are still commoners today, and status is granted through land registered under the Commons Registration Act of 1965. Anyone can become a commoner by buying particular land near the forest. Commoners have long grazed livestock, cut trees for firewood, scythed bracken for the bedding of livestock, and periodically burned vegetation. In the past, commoners also had the right to pasture pigs, the right to cut turf or peat for fuel, the right to fish

LEFT **Thomas Friend, a commoner of Ashdown Forest, carrying a short faggot of wood in the 1890s**

ABOVE **Friend returns to work.**

Gills Lap from Colemans Hatch, Ashdown

The mark of human history on the barren forest, Gills Lap from Colemans Hatch, 1890–1910

RIGHT **Roots of a beech tree clutch the pale boundary.**

lakes, ponds, or streams, and the right to take stone or soil for use on the commonable holding. Today, in designated areas and at set times of year, 730 commoners may still exercise their Right of Estovers (gathering wood) in basic form: cutting birch, willow, or alder for use in the ancestral hearth. Commoners are entitled to two cords of wood per year. Over the centuries, this foraging and gathering inhibited scrub and woodland and contributed to the forest we see today.

From Wasteland to Jewel in the Crown

The common land provided the resources that people depended on every day, including home heat sources and bedding for their animals. Plucky commoners fought for their rights to the common land despite threats from the late nineteenth-century Earl De La Warr. Indeed, while the countryside surrounding Ashdown Forest is a scene of pastoral English beauty—soft green hills, small farms and clusters of woods—centuries of use by commoners created a depleted moonscape. The impact on the landscape was recorded by the well-traveled William Cobbett, a famous English journalist, pamphleteer, and chronicler of nineteenth-century agrarian life in England. In 1822, Cobbett rode through the forest and wrote impressions in his book, *Rural Rides*:

> At about three miles from Grinstead you come to a pretty village, called Forest-Row and then, on the road to Uckfield, you cross Ashurst (sic) Forest, which is a heath, with here and there a few birch scrubs upon it, verily the most villainously ugly spot I saw in England. This lasts you for five miles, getting, if possible, uglier and uglier all the way, till, at last, as if barren soil, nasty spewy gravel, heath and even that stunted, were not enough, you see some rising spots, which instead of trees, present you with black, ragged, hideous rocks.

Kidd's Hill in
Ashdown Forest,
about 1900

He was not a fan. If alive today to ride trails through the forest, Cobbett would be delighted to see how England's "most villainously ugly spot" has regenerated and is now a highly protected East Sussex jewel. Indeed its shape is like an Old European diamond, an inverted triangle seven miles tip-to-tip from east to west and roughly the same distance north to south. Like gems in the Tower of London, the forest is surrounded by a fortress of legal protections. These safeguard it as a large continuous heathland supporting rare species of flora and fauna. Today if Cobbett could walk the white sand paths on Gills Lap in August and look toward the South Down hills and English Channel, he would see a pink and maroon carpet of iconic forest heather, a landscape transformed by commoners, as well as nibblers like deer and rabbit, into a place of international ecological significance.

Decades before Piglet picked violets for Eeyore and Tigger climbed a Scots pine with Roo, a Board of Conservators was created to manage the forest. Since 1885, this body has protected the rights of commoners as well as guarding the forest from development,

preserving its natural heathland and woodland beauty. There are also national and international designations. In recent decades, Natural England, the public body that advises the UK government on the natural environment and countryside, has designated the forest as a "Site of Special Scientific Interest," highlighting it an important wildlife site. It is among the largest continuous areas of heathland, semi-natural woodland, and valley bogs in southeast England. The EU has also conferred designations on the forest. It is a Special Protection Area on account of its having the haunting nocturnal nightjar and more than 1 percent of the United Kingdom's breeding populations of the jaunty Dartford warbler, which plummeted in the UK to a few pairs in the 1960s and has resurged thanks to habitat restoration and growth.

The forest is also classified as a Special Area of Conservation, a network of protected habitats across the European Union. Ashdown Forest was awarded this status on account of its heaths which provide habitat for beetles, dragonflies, damselflies, and butterflies including the nationally rare silver-studded blue. If you look

Atmospheric woods surround Ashdown Forest.

closely, you can see these special creatures in Shepard's drawings, where dragonflies and butterflies flutter and hover over streams and in the woods, and are a part of Rabbit's large band of friends and relations.

The forest is also part of the High Weald Area of Outstanding Natural Beauty. One step down from a national park and one of forty-one sites in England and Wales, it is, as its name suggests, a distinctive and protected landscape of natural beauty. Ashdown Forest is particularly noted for its biodiversity, rare and diverse species, and the ancient and interconnected habitats that support them.

In addition, and in response to regional, national, and international protections, the local Wealden District Council has created a four-mile zone around the forest to limit damage and disturbance of this important habitat. The idea is to reduce pressure and development in housing, retail, and economic activities close to the forest, as well as monitoring air quality and the impact of increased traffic on nitrogen deposition within habitats, plant communities, and plant species.

A patchwork of
small farms in the
High Weald Area
of Outstanding
Natural Beauty

The laws all preserve the biodiversity of Ashdown Forest. And in doing so, the literary landscape of the Hundred Acre Wood is also protected. The legacy of Milne and his village of Hartfield could have easily been commercially exploited, given the enduring appeal and worldwide recognition of *Winnie-the-Pooh* and *The House at Pooh Corner*. Delightfully, this has not happened. If anything, it is hard to discern that this area was the inspiration for what has become an iconic literary setting. Visitors come to the forest with honey and Heffalumps on their minds, but it is hard to find footprints of Pooh, Piglet, Roo, and their friends. (That is, except once, when I was hiking and an adult wearing a giant Tigger onesie came around a bend in the trail. Beware: such creatures do indeed roam the forest at-large.) Still, nothing is garish, nothing is overt. A couple of demure signs point the way to Poohsticks Bridge. In the forest, the way to the Milne and Shepard stone memorial is deliberately unmarked so that people can discover it on their own (or by following a walk on a brochure). And so, protecting the environment also preserves warm childhood memories.

The Story Underfoot

The top of the Hundred Acre Wood is where Christopher Robin lives in a house with a green door. Here in the depths of Ashdown Forest, you can't find a tree with a door—that is for you to discover near Poohsticks Bridge—but it is quiet up here, as if the whole world were sleeping behind a door. At the top of the forest on a clear day, sunshine dances through trees and warblers bob between gorse bushes. Here the sky spreads an inviting blanket of blue for us to daydream and cloud watch, remember our own childhoods and hold the hands of our own children.

Peering through a window from his bedroom at Cotchford Farm, Milne's son Christopher Robin could see trees swaying on top of Gills Lap two miles to the south. In the stories, the animals live throughout the forest, but memorable events take place on a high, sandy plateau of gorse and heather as if it were Grand Central Station. For example, Roo is kidnapped here. Tigger scrambles up a tree here, though he forgets he must also come down. Pooh rolls in mud and clings to a blue balloon, all in search of honey. And after Pooh rescues Piglet from the flood, Christopher Robin assembles a table out of wood and throws a special party here for the Brave Bear, bestowing upon him a Special Pencil Case with little pockets for Green Pencils, Blue Pencils, and Red Pencils, as well as an India rubber and a ruler for words to walk on.

Walking on the fine white sand here feels like sifting through magic pixie dust. But the story underfoot is not merely fictional; it is a layered geological one. The geology explains why the setting looks the way it does, why particular plants grow here, and how that Dartford warbler, among other animals, came to chatter in the gorse. It also explains how the gorse popped onto the scene in the first place.

Here the forest sits atop some of the highest ground in the High Weald. While the forest floor is white sand, other parts are brown ground, and in some places the color of paprika. These are bands of sandstone and clay, both of which were originally muddy and

The geology underfoot on Broadstone Warren

Hard sandstone outcrops

sandy sediments. These were formed by the hard, thin sandstone which runs east–west while the softer clay has weathered, creating steep valleys in between. Rivers such as the Medway and Ouse have helped shape the earth, cutting through the landscape to create ravines known as "ghylls" (pronounced "gills").

Sediments that formed at the bottoms of lakes were deposited by rivers 140 million years ago. When sea levels rose 100 million years ago, the remains of billions of sea creatures, which eventually became chalk, left another layer. A giant chalk-covered dome popped up 30 million years ago. This has been eroded away by water over time to reveal the clay and sandstone strata—the High and Low Weald. The hardest sandstone, which has withstood weathering, can be seen in the squat, characterful sandstone outcrops.

This geology in turn affects what grows in Ashdown Forest. It affects which animals will call it home and what people have done

here as well. Away from Gills Lap, in the woods where there are streams, stop and look into the water that Milne writes about with such tenderness. These ghylls are steep-sided, often with red-stained channels hinting at another significant part of the landscape story—the iron industry: its extraction, the massive cutting of ancient trees to fuel the smelting, and the damming of rivers. There were two main periods of iron-production in the forest: between the first and third centuries AD when the Romans improved and expanded the existing bloomeries (small furnaces) and the Tudor and Stuart times. You can see archaeological evidence of this just south of Gills Lap on the main road between London and the town of Lewes. Pull into the Roman Road car park and look north toward Gills Lap. What looks like a mound for rabbits is actually a partly metaled Roman road created with used slag, or molten waste material.

A golf course designed by nature, the heath-covered Royal Ashdown Forest Golf Club is a Top 100 course with challenges of heather, narrow fairways, streams and hollows.

LEFT A wooded ghyll stream

Bluebells carpet an ancient path where over centuries herds
of animals were led from one food source to another.

A gill stream

Flora of the Forest

There's an Old English folk saying: "When gorse is out of bloom, kissing is out of season." Which is to say, when the January sun is hidden behind a shroud of clouds and a mixture of brown bracken and heather extends across the forest, there are always yellow gorse flowers—even if they come wrapped in packages of razor-sharp leaves in intimidating thickets. Downhill in Daphne's garden at Cotchford Farm, flowers begin to shake their sleepy heads in February, with daffodils and pink flowers of quince surrounding the farmhouse.

What grows in Daphne's old gardens and the village of Hartfield are of course domesticated spaces—not what you will see in the forest. The forest is wild and fresh, quiet in song and subdued in appearance October through April. Villagers hang baskets of smiling pansies, their flowery faces peering over the wire rims like Roo from Kanga's pouch. In the cemetery, swathes of snowdrops, shaped like Victorian lampshades, flow through grass, rippling around mossy headstones in the shadow of the steeple.

Forest flora is slower to wake in spring than their imported cousins in the village. However, come April in Wrens Warren Valley, a dozen shades of green transform the landscape as trees, shrubs, and grasses awaken. When you take a walk in the forest, look down in meadows to see tiny red berries glistening like Christmas ornaments on bilberry shrubs. Wild daffodils are waning then and ferns are emerging in the shape of hearts.

In the forest, the three main ecological habitats are heathland, woodland, and streams and ponds. The lowland heathlands are rare and threatened, and have greatly declined in the last two centuries. In England, it is thought that only one-sixth of the heathland present in 1800 remains. And of Ashdown's ten square miles, heathland comprises 60 percent of the landscape while woodland covers the remaining 40 percent. In Ashdown Forest there are four thousand acres of heathland, made up largely of ling, bracken, bell heather, and two species of gorse. There are scattered trees and

Forming an impenetrable thicket on heathland, European gorse flowers
from winter through early summer, giving way to dwarf gorse, a smaller and
more delicate plant which flowers July to September.

Scots pine and
European gorse
in spring

scrub, areas of bare ground, wet heaths, bogs, and open water.
Heathlands range from wet to dry, with dry heathlands on high,
wind-swept hills and wet ones in iron-rich valley bogs, an intricate
mosaic of plants in different conditions. In drier areas of the forest,
few plants can compete with ling as it thrives in acid soils and
shades out other plants. Dwarf gorse is a small low shrub that
blooms July through September. Next to pink-purple bell heather,
the gorse creates a visually rich tapestry of purple and gold.

Along the edge of damp heath areas, the pretty blue marsh gen-
tian, one of the forest's most famous yet scarce plants, signals its
presence with bright blue trumpet flowers. Like the dwarf gorse, it
flowers from July through October and is found only in about a

dozen colonies. Where the water table hovers within a few inches of the surface, deer grass and sphagnum mosses grow. There are also two species of beautiful scarlet-colored sundews, *Drosera rotundi-folia* and *D. intermedia*, which caught the attention of Charles Darwin in 1860 when he visited his sister-in-law who lived near Colemans Hatch in the forest. The sundews fascinated Darwin to such an extent that his wife could be forgiven for thinking they captured the man himself. It did result in his taking several samples to his home and ultimately writing his 1875 *Insectivorous Plants*, the first well-known dissertation on carnivorous plants. In fact, the book opens with a passage about the sundews he studied here in Ashdown Forest.

Indeed, the moist areas on the heathland contain plants which are abundant on many of the moorlands of northern and western Britain, but are rare or very rare in southeast England. This includes the delicate white beak sedge, common cotton grass, and bog asphodel. On a late June walk in Broadstone Valley, botanist Hew Prendergast introduced me to clusters of sundews growing in a small bog on a grassy slope. Without a trained eye, they can be hard to spot. But kneeling, I could see this colony of sundews was thriving, tentacles of each plant glistening as sticky secretions caught the sunlight, and plastered in flies and ants. Nearby, spears of delicate yellow bog asphodel bobbed in the tall summer grasses.

Gorse makes an appearance in the "Expotition to the North Pole." Christopher Robin pauses at a twist in a river and surveys potential dangers.

> "It's just the place," he explained, "for an Ambush."
> "What sort of bush?" whispered Pooh to Piglet. "A gorse-bush?"
> "My dear Pooh," said Owl in his superior way, "don't you know what an Ambush is?"
> "Owl," said Piglet, looking at him severely, "Pooh's whisper was a perfectly private whisper, and there was no need—"

"An ambush," said Owl, "is a sort of Surprise."

"So is a gorse-bush sometimes," said Pooh.

"An Ambush, as I was about to explain to Pooh," said Piglet, "is a sort of Surprise."

"If people jump out at you suddenly, that's an Ambush," said Owl.

"It's an Ambush, Pooh, when people jump at you suddenly," explained Piglet.

Pooh, who now knew what an Ambush was, said that a gorse-bush had sprung at him suddenly one day when he fell off a tree, and he had taken six days to get all the prickles out of himself.

"We are not talking about gorse-bushes," said Owl a little crossly.

"I am," said Pooh.

The heathland in the forest is a "plagioclimax" type. This simply means that it originated through human activity and is maintained by human activity. To maintain the heathland, the Conservators of Ashdown Forest engage in management practices which mimic activities of commoners, including regularly cutting bracken and felling trees to prevent the loss of open heathland. If they ceased these activities, the landscape would revert to woodland. Commoners still do have rights to cut for wood, but even collectively so, it is not enough to maintain such a large heathland.

To the occasional dismay and protestations of people unfamiliar with the management practices and conservation vision of Ashdown Forest, rangers use chainsaws and tractors to cut trees and mow bracken. It is meant to mimic the activities of people and animals on the land: nibbling, collecting, burning. Today, there has been a return to natural grazers, with small herds of Exmoor ponies, Galloway cattle, and Hebridean sheep. They keep emerging bracken, birch, and other plants in check and help maintain a heathland that supports rare plants, birds, and invertebrates.

Exmoor ponies in
Wrens Warren Valley

LEFT The forest's
Hebridean sheep on
temporary rented
pasture

Charles Darwin and Sundews

IN THE SUMMER OF 1860, the year after *On the Origin of Species* was published, Darwin escaped from the scientific battles over his book to the open space of Ashdown Forest with his family. He stayed at The Ridge, the Colemans Hatch home of Sarah Elizabeth Wedgewood, the sister of his wife, Emma. There he im mersed himself in botanical studies, especially with the carnivorous sundew, *Drosera rotundifolia*. He collected specimens not far from The Ridge and took them back to his greenhouses at Down House where he conducted a number of experiments on them.

In *Wives of Fame*, author Edna Healey writes how Emma was relieved he had something other than his book to worry about. In a letter to the wife of Charles Lyell, Darwin's fierce advocate, Emma wrote, "At present, he is treating *Drosera* just like a living creature, and I suppose he hopes to end in proving it to be an animal."

Today, less than a mile west of The Ridge—perhaps in the neighborhood where Darwin explored—there grows a patch of sundews in ideal conditions: a seasonally moist habitat in acidic soil with ample sunlight. Like a carpet of striking rubies, the tiny plants glisten as if they were dripping with dew in the sun. But it is deceiving. The dew is not sweet. It is living fly paper. The tentacles are sticky

Intermediate-leaved sundew, *Drosera intermedia*

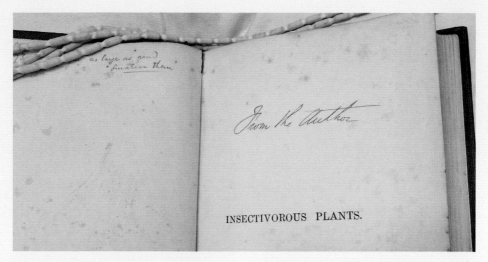

INSECTIVOROUS PLANTS.

"Drawings of *Drosera* and *Dionaea*, given in this work, were made for me by my son George Darwin."

with goo, which arrests and absorbs insects attracted to the sparkling light. The more the insect struggles, the tighter the sundew's grip becomes. The prey—flies, ants, damselflies, and especially mosquitoes that emerge from nearby bogs—supplement the sundew's mineral-poor diet. Unlike the Venus flytrap, which slams its door on its prey without a moment of hesitation, *Drosera* plants are more languid. Depending on the struggle it senses, a plant may take its time rolling up its leaf edges—sometimes curling 180 degrees in a minute when presented with an especially panicky mosquito, or several minutes for a more fatalistic fly which has less fight in it. The enzymes in the sticky fluid of *Drosera* tentacles first drown the insect, then break down and sop up its body as a delicious nitrogen-rich meal.

Fig. 1.*
(*Drosera rotundifolia.*)
Leaf viewed from above; enlarged four times.

Flowers in the Forest

MILNE WAS AN ATTENTIVE LISTENER, not just to people but to the sounds, colors, and rhythms of seasons. From his boyhood walking adventures with Ken to ambling Ashdown Forest with Christopher Robin, he drew inspiration for the ways his characters felt as well. Here, Pooh is in the company of two friends, but the summer scents of flowers and buzzing of bees draw his attention elsewhere.

One day Rabbit and Piglet were sitting outside Pooh's front door listening to Rabbit, and Pooh was sitting with them. It was a drowsy summer afternoon, and the Forest was full of gentle sounds, which all seemed to be saying to Pooh, "Don't listen to Rabbit, listen to me."

—From "*In Which* Tigger Is Unbounced," *The House at Pooh Corner*

Cross-leaved heath coming into flower in June atop Gills Lap

The unfurling of bracken (*Pteridium aquilinum*)

Bilberry (*Vaccinium myrtillus*)

Wild daffodil in Wrens Warren Valley

Bog asphodel (*Narthecium ossifragum*) flourishing in damp heath

Summer bumblebees in foxgloves (*Digitalis purpurea*)

Heath spotted orchid (*Dactylorhiza maculata*)

Cross-leaved heath (*Erica tetralix*)

Bog cotton grass (*Eriophorum angustifolium*)

Purple moor-grass (*Molinea caerulea*), a dominant grass on the heathland

Wet and boggy heathland

Bracken is one of the most widespread plants in the world and historically significant in the forest.

Bracken and cross-leaved heath

Woodlands and Streams

Trees growing in the nearby Five Hundred Acre Wood are older than those growing in the woods of Ashdown Forest, where the woodlands are mainly post–World War II, and largely composed of silver birch, English oak, and Scots pine. There are also lines of beech marking old pale boundaries as well as areas of coppiced sweet chestnut, a tree introduced to England by the Romans. Coppicing is a traditional English approach of cutting trees to the stump every eight to ten years and exploiting the new growth. The once-thriving hop industry of Sussex and Kent heavily relied on coppiced chestnuts for long straight poles to support the growing plants. The industry has since faded, but multiple-stemmed chestnuts can still be seen when you walk in the woods. Today their main use is in the fence palings which can be seen around Sussex. A fine example of an idiosyncratic Sussex fencing style can be seen in front of the Ashdown Forest Centre.

As Christopher Milne tells us in his autobiography, he often played in the Five Hundred Acre Wood—alone, with Nanny in sight, or with the future tenth Earl De La Warr, who was a year younger than Christopher Robin. We know the trees he climbed in the Five Hundred Acre Wood were models for many of the homes inhabited by Pooh and friends. Over the ridge of Wrens Warren Valley grew a grove of giant chestnut trees upon which Owl's house, The Chestnuts, was modeled. As we learned earlier, those trees, like Owl's own house, blew down in World War II.

Though the ancient chestnuts that Christopher Robin climbed are gone, many glorious trees still stand for us to enjoy. The "Tabell Ghyll" walking brochure from the Forest Centre will lead you along several areas of coppiced chestnuts and then further down to an open magical place where a majestic beech tree towers over birch and bracken. It is hard to miss it in this quiet woodland setting. If you have children scampering along with you, they may find an Eeyore house made of branches in the understory. Pause here. This may be one of the most unforgettable natural playgrounds you will encounter with your children.

Birch, beech, snags, and oak

Juvenile tawny owl in oak tree

You will also see notable trees in other places. Within the first five minutes of the "Broadstone Amble" walk from the Forest Centre, you will encounter a line of beech, a common boundary tree of the time, with roots still clutching the 1685 pale boundary like owl talons on a branch. If ever a tree knew how to keep things in line, the tall, stately, and strong beeches here still delineate the old pale. The trees makes superb history lessons for children as well.

Throughout these walks and on others, you will find myriad other trees as well, including oak, alder, hazel, and holly. You may also see hazel coppices. These provide homes for the dormouse and plants including butchers broom, a low evergreen shrub with medicinal red berries. Spring and summer walks in the woods provide opportunities to see shade-loving plants such as bluebells, which begin to emerge in the woods of Ashdown Forest in mid-April and electrify English woodlands by late April. In the cool, dappled light of the woods, pretty wood anemone, wood sorrel, and common cow-wheat grow as well.

The Ashdown Forest Centre booklets include plant identifications. Young adventurers enjoying a day of picnicking, Poohsticks, and Expotitions may find identifying plants a new and exciting challenge. It may make it even more fun for them to learn that the author of the *Winnie-the-Pooh* stories they so love was a keen young naturalist, as was Christopher Robin—the fictional character as well as the real boy whose quiet curiosities about the world around him inspired the stories. Share with your children the story of the toad that Milne and Ken "collected" and stories of his other natural curiosities. Describe how unusually far he wandered as a child. Ask them if they would like to do the same. Where would they go if they could? Explain how Milne moved to the forest to give Christopher Robin, one of the most famous children in the world in the late 1920s, the kind of childhood he experienced himself, and how these experiences led to stories embraced by people around the world.

Silver birch (*Betula pendula*) and bracken

Greater stitchwort (*Stellaria holostea*)

Bluebell (*Hyacinthoides non-scripta*)

Lords-and-ladies or cuckoo-pint
(*Arum maculatum*)

Foxgloves (*Digitalis purpurea*) in the woods

And of course, bring your own copies of the original *Winnie-the-Pooh* and *The House at Pooh Corner* to read in an Eeyore house, in a Thoughtful Spot, or in the Enchanted Place. They are all over the forest.

Whenever the muse came to him, which was quite often, Winnie-the-Pooh loved to hum and sing, walk, and write poetry about friendships and nature. Here, in the first two stanzas of a poem written by Pooh in "*In Which* Rabbit Has a Busy Day," spring emerges in the forest. Butterflies, primroses, violets, and turtle doves that populate the poem are flora and fauna Milne would have seen as he walked in the woods and heather.

NOISE, BY POOH

Oh, the butterflies are flying,
Now the winter days are dying,
And the primroses are trying
    To be seen.

And the turtle-doves are cooing,
And the woods are up and doing,
For the violets are blue-ing
    In the green.

On the Table Ghyll walk, look for this beech (*Fagus sylvatica*).

Piglet picks a spring bouquet for Eeyore.

Piglet had got up early that morning to pick himself a bunch of violets; and when he had picked them and put them in a pot in the middle of his house, it suddenly came over him that nobody had ever picked Eeyore a bunch of violets, and the more he thought of this, the more he thought how sad it was to be an Animal who had never had a bunch of violets picked for him.

—"*In Which* Rabbit Has a Busy Day, and We Learn What Christopher Robin Does in the Mornings," *The House at Pooh Corner*

A native violet (*Viola* species) and primrose (*Primula vulgaris*)

Tree Clumps in the Forest

Tree clumps were useful as blinds for hunters and shelter for game. Were these the reasons for the clusters of trees we see dotted around the forest? For at least one, named King's Standing, that is indeed the case. King Henry VIII likely trotted down to Ashdown Forest for a couple of his famous uber-manly pursuits: to chase deer and the dear Anne Boleyn, the vivacious lover he wooed at Bolebroke Castle, a circa 1480 hunting lodge two miles north of Hartfield near her family home, Hever Castle, in neighboring Kent. When the tenor of their relationship, shall we say, "wavered," should we ask what he was doing on the morning of her execution? Ladies—brace yourselves—he was *hunting* with his mates.

A purported hunting blind or hide at one time, King's Standing is where Henry VIII—seated, not actually standing, given what we

The history of Hartfield is engraved in its village sign.

know of his big appetites and corresponding girth—likely waited with a longbow or crossbow at the ready while his beaters drove the quarry of deer toward him. Given the theatrical nature of the hunt, we can imagine that at a particular signal—like "Action!" on a stage—deer were let loose to run in front of the king. The hope was that, with incredible luck and a keen eye, the king would shoot into the heart of a stag (though, of course, a hazard of signing up to be a beater meant you yourself could also be struck by errant bolts). Very few shots would have brought down an animal straight away. Well-trained dogs would thus be brought in to chase down the stricken quarry.

The heritage and history of the deer hunt are commemorated in Hartfield's wrought iron village sign. Throughout England, these decorative pictograms announce to those entering the village what the local area is about. For Hartfield, the stag is key. In the Domesday Book of 1086—a great survey of the worth of each landholder's livestock and land, which was ordered by William the Conqueror—the name "Hartfield" is then known as "Hertevel" and "hertefeld," meaning "the open land frequented by stags." It originates from a combination of the Old English pre-seventh-century words "heorot" (meaning hart and stag) and "feld" (meaning pasture or open country).

A description of Hartfield from the Domesday Book

Kings Standing and the Enchanted Place are two of many tree clumps dotting the forest landscape. Like ink drops on the parchment paper of the white sandy heathland, the clumps, we might guess, could have been planted by manly men on the orders of a king keen on hunting. Not so. Who planted them and why is a curious story. Perhaps they were indeed practical features, for purposes of navigation, or maybe they were a decorative element in this stark landscape. However, there is more to the story of The Enchanted Place than the friendship between a boy and his bear. It involves a friendship between a countess and a queen.

And the story goes like this. The De La Warr family owns the Five Hundred Acre Wood. (Their ancestor, Sir Thomas West—Lord De La Warr—was the governor of the English colony at Jamestown, Virginia, in 1610 and "Delaware" originates from their French family name.) Located along the northeast side of Ashdown Forest near the village of Withyham, Buckhurst, the family estate, has been owned by the De La Warrs and Sackvilles for nine hundred years. The Five Hundred Acre Wood inspired Milne to create the Hundred Acre Wood. Christopher Robin fished and played there in the 1920s and '30s with William Sackville, Lord Buckhurst, later the tenth Earl De La Warr, and his younger brother, the Honorable Harry Sackville. Elizabeth, Countess De La Warr, inherited Buckhurst from her brother. She lived from 1795 to 1870 and planted the first of these clumps on hilltops beginning in 1825. An heiress of a then vast estate and fortune, Countess Elizabeth also planted trees in the garden at Buckhurst.

Although she is recognized for planting these clusters on the landscape, Countess Elizabeth's reasons for *doing so* have not been fully explored. Perhaps from windows at Buckhurst there were sightlines across the landscape she wanted to mark. Maybe she planted them to help people navigate around the forest since evergreens, especially when closely planted, can be seen for miles. Dr. Hew Prendergast, director of the Conservators of Ashdown Forest from 2003 to 2011 and previously at the Royal Botanic Gardens Kew, said:

Gills Lap, Ashdown Forest.

**The Enchanted Place,
tree clump, 1900**

To have an evergreen tree in the landscape would be something different from the predominant deciduous trees. Apart from the yew tree, which is not uncommon around here, it is possible a Scots pine was selected because it was effectively *on* a treeless landscape. The very existence of trees at the tops of hills would have made a big visual impact. And the fact that people didn't like them is quite an interesting statement in itself.

As it happened, Countess De La Warr's enthusiasm for decorating or navigating was not altogether shared: a number of tree clusters originally planted by her were ripped out by plucky commoners who felt she was intruding on their space. The Enchanted Place and Kings Standing are believed to be original tree clumps, with new Scots pines planted by rangers when occasional trees die.

The choice of tree is interesting. Perhaps Countess Elizabeth chose Scots pine over the more common native yew (*Taxus baccata*) because she preferred the pine's form and growth over other evergreens available in the British Isles at the time. With its long, bare trunk, distinctive habit, and flat-topped, rounded foliage, clusters of Scots pines have a different impact on the horizon than a single and slightly unwieldy evergreen yew. Yew is also considered suitable for formal gardens or church yards, and, as the Countess Anne De La Warr suggested, "would have been a very unlikely plant for someone from Countess Elizabeth's background to plant in a forest."

The yew was omnipresent yet distinguished for many reasons: the hardest of the softwoods, it had been used in spears, long bows, and musical instruments. Rather than surrender, Celtic leaders including Eburones chief Catuvolcus and the Orosius and Cantabrian tribes took their own lives by sword, by fire, and sometimes by extract of yew. Compared to the slow-growing yew, which reaches 400 to 600 years old (with a few noteworthy exceptions at 1500 to 3000 years old), Scots pines live just 150 to 300 years. In other words, pines are quick and yews are slow. Countess Elizabeth's tree options were also limited before the great wave of conifer introductions by plant hunters.

Despite these limitations, she had other reasons to choose it. Countess Elizabeth was on very close terms with Queen Victoria, twenty-four years her junior. "A close connection with Queen Elizabeth I was established through a marriage with a Boleyn girl," says Buckhurst literature, "And the Queen soon promoted her cousin Thomas Sackville to the titles Lord Buckhurst and Earl of Dorset, later to become Dukes of Dorset and Earls De La Warr." Centuries later, the connection between the families continues to be cultivated through tree planting at Buckhurst, a tradition started by Elizabeth and Queen Victoria who planted an English oak, a tree symbolizing strength and endurance. King Edward VII planted a

Buckhurst was originally built in 1602 with golden sandstone from a local quarry.

cedar, Her Majesty Queen Elizabeth the Queen Mother a copper beech, HRH Princess Margaret a lime, and recently the Duchess of Cornwall planted another oak in Buckhurst's Diamond Jubilee Wood to commemorate the Diamond Jubilee of Elizabeth II.

A keen historian, the Countess Anne De La Warr reflected on the relationship between the queen and the countess. "Countess Elizabeth was very interested in Buckhurst Estate and managed the place well," she said, looking through open doors at Buckhurst across green hills where Shetland ponies grazed. A view once enjoyed by Queen Victoria, today it looks out to a serene garden created by the Countess Anne De La Warr, a space with mounded boxwoods, frothy geraniums, purple catnip, and pale yellow lady's mantle.

On a tour of Buckhurst, as the Countess De La Warr reflected on what motivated her predecessor, we were driven down a dirt road, through gate after gate, toward the grove where Christopher Robin played as a little boy. "Friendship with the queen would have

A humble setting
for a queen's tea

counted for a lot," she said, pondering the origins of the tree clumps. We passed a small wooden barn. "There, for example, is where Queen Victoria and the countess had tea. She and Countess Elizabeth were picnicking. It started raining and that's where they found shelter."

As for the particular choice of Scots pine, which are staples in Shepard's illustrations of the Hundred Acre Wood, imagine a friend is coming to visit. You know she takes pleasure in peonies and roses. You want to welcome her, to let her know you're thinking of her. You set out fragrant bouquets of peonies and roses where she will enjoy them—in a sunny window, on her night table, at the dining table. As the Earl De La Warr suggested, the clumps may have been created by the countess as "marks of respect for her friend, the monarch." After our tour of Buckhurst, we sat at the table in their kitchen, talking about trees and queens and countesses. The doors were opened onto the landscape, a view framed by climbing roses, and the Countess De La Warr said after some thought, "If you like

The Earl De La Warr with an 1810 portrait of Elizabeth, Countess De La Warr

someone and you enjoy spending time with them, it's a way of expressing that."

The Scots pines had symbolism and sentiment as well. Queen Victoria and Prince Albert had both fallen in love with Scotland. They loved the rolling hills and pine trees, which reminded Albert of his native Coburg, Germany, which the queen also loved and called her second home. They bought Balmoral Castle in 1848 and it was referred to as her "dear paradise in the Highlands." The queen's obsession with Scotland—she dressed her sons in tartan kilts and Balmoral is saturated in tartan even to this day—influenced her richer subjects, who all rushed off there for holidays. It is likely that Countess De La Warr's planting of Scots pines were grand sentimental gestures for her friend Queen Victoria. Can there be any more fitting origins for the Enchanted Place than a real-life friendship?

Birds in the Forest

On winter days, the high heathland of the forest may seem as inviting as the bottom of a cold, dark Heffalump trap. But there are clear blue days when an empty quietude settles over faded heathers, dry grass, and wind-blown woodlands. On days like this, there is such clarity in the cold, crisp air that you feel you could skip a stone across the English Channel to the northern shores of France. There is less of everything then: color, movement, light, and visitors—including those of the feathered sort. Birds—some common, some rare—winter on the Continent while others find the open heather and woods of Ashdown Forest a less competitive, more comfortable winter home. There may be less, indeed, but there is also more: more breathing room, longer shadows, and windier wind through woodlands.

Bright February mornings are not rare and are a fine time to visit the forest. One such morning, I walked down the dirt lane from Cotchford Farm to Poohsticks Bridge. A path veers off the lane to the bridge. The canopy of trees covering the path had been severely cut since my last visit in October. It would all indeed grow back, but branches touching overhead had once created a magical tunnel of dappled light to a treasured site. Miffed, I walked the little way downhill to Poohsticks Bridge with a little grey cloud over my head. I brought six sticks and played three rounds of Poohsticks with myself—a bit daft, left hand versus right. The river kneaded the banks, swirling and twisting with eddies and currents, and the game went fast.

Mind on the water, I leaned against the wooden rail of the bridge. Soon my senses shifted from looking at water currents to listening to wood songs. As I stood on the bridge, the sticks long downriver, I realized these winter woods were alive with crystalline and rhythmic songs. There were liquid drops and raspy whistles, staccato calls and low chock-chock-chocks. A male English robin, far more smartly dressed than I, settled on the opposite rail, and we assessed each other's outdoor fashion, bemused. I walked back along the path and, despite the severe cutting, listened to the lively presence of song thrushes, wood pigeons, sparrows, magpies, and crows. Families of foraging blue tits, a colorful blend of blue, green, yellow, and white, hopped between and hung upside down from tree branches in search of food. There is a lot of life in the forest in winter if you slow your pace, look, and listen.

Whether walking in the heather or woods, there are some tips to enhance your birding experience whether you are alone or with your children. Bring a field guide and binoculars to better see and identify birds. Carry a notebook to sketch different patterns and colors on birds you see. Practice good fieldcraft by moving slowly and quietly, and avoid wearing bright colors. Listen to bird calls and songs as you walk or sit in one place. Settle yourself to see both resident and wintering birds nearby in the woods and heathlands.

Atop trees, you might glimpse two speckled, upright thrushes—the fieldfare and redwing—whose fluty songs are a mellifluous joy in winter. They are common winter visitors but are rare breeding birds in the United Kingdom. A third thrush—the big, bold mistle thrush—is a year-round resident. All three thrushes feed on berries, fruits, and invertebrates, roosting in the later afternoons.

A member of the finch family, the brambling breeds in Scandinavia and western Siberia, and winters across Europe, including the forest. Like the thrushes, they can be seen on the edges of woodlands. Recognizable males in orange and white can be seen in big flocks. Not much larger than a blackbird, the great grey shrike, a beautiful bird with white-grey plumage and a black mask, is a wintry delight to humans, but altogether something else to other birds. A fascinating mini-predator to watch, it hunts beetles, voles, and mice, along with other birds such as greenfinches, storing its prey in little larders on impaled thorns.

These cold-weather beauties disappear when temperatures rise. Come spring, there is a dramatic influx of birds diverse in color, habit, song, and size. Birdsong is best at dawn when birds sing to affirm their territories before foraging. The air is also denser then and carries song farther, an asset for both birds and birders. A particularly melodious bird to listen for is the dappled woodlark, a protected heathland specialty, which prefers the open areas of grazed heathers and gorse as well as open woodland. It has a sweet song of whistles and a distinct "titloo-eet" call. The stonechat, as its name suggests, sounds like two stones tapping together. The male looks especially smart in its russet vest and black overcoat. When birding in the forest, the magic happens when you stop trying so hard to find something. On a June hike in woodlands near Linton car park, for example, I was stumping along, feeling free and easy like Pooh, but still looking for an adventure to come my way. It was mid-day. I had seen many forest birds and butterflies flutter past me. But a sudden *whooshing* feeling came over me, perhaps a bit like Eeyore when hooshed by Tigger into the stream. Three juvenile

Short-toed eagle on a successful hunt for adders in Wrens Warren Valley

BELOW **Thousands of "twitchers" flocked to the forest to glimpse a rare short-toed eagle on Gills Lap, June 2014.**

tawny owls had been perching together like the Three Musketeers on the branch of a fat oak and—as startled by me as I was by them—two had just taken flight. To my delight, one owl remained, blinking at me for one long minute. I snapped a picture, and then it took wing into the green light of summer woodlands.

In the cool blue winter light, lesser redpolls may be seen on silver birch catkins. Siskins feed on alder seeds and often are seen hanging upside down from them like trapeze artists. There may also be crossbills, their presence notable by falling debris from pine trees. In the forest, Greenwood Gate and Wrens Warren are recommended areas to see them. Reed buntings call the forest home all year and are most populous in winter months. With unmistakable bright yellow heads and underbellies, yellowhammers sing from low bushes in spring and summer. The common redstart needs tree

Dartford warbler

Cuckoo

Redstart

Wheatear

Firecrest

Turtle dove

holes for nesting and they are often seen at the bottom of the old airstrip in the forest. And even for short periods, it is delightful to watch brownish-grey spotted flycatchers, their fly-catching tricks amusing to adult and children as they dart from their perches to grab a flying insect and return to the same spot.

The dappled grey and chestnut turtle dove, sadly in decline, returns to the forest with a distinctive purring. The best place to see them in the forest is Duddleswell and Airman's Grave. The familiar song of the sleek grey cuckoo, also waning in numbers, can be heard throughout the day from dawn to early evening. They are familiar brood-parasites, the females laying their eggs in the nests of other birds. There are so many other birds to see and hear, including larger birds of prey such as kestrels, buzzards, and the occasional red kite, as well as unusual headline-makers like the juvenile short-toed eagle that was blown off-course to Ashdown Forest from Africa in 2014. And a special summer treat that cannot be missed is the nocturnal nightjar. Like the cuckoo, its wings are pointed and its tail is long, and its mottled brown plumage provides camouflage in daylight. Old folk tales, which purport that the bird steals milk from goats, has given the bird a mystical reputation. Take time for a heathland walk at dusk to hear this rare and haunting bird. The next morning, get out early to hear as many songbirds at dawn as possible. It will be an unforgettable experience.

Nightjar

A Game in the Woods

Never has there been a bridge as iconic and humble as Poohsticks Bridge. A short walk down the lane from Cotchford Farm, the wooden bridge extends across a tributary to the Medway in a quiet, shady place in the woods. Between 1925 and 1940, it was often visited by Christopher Robin and his father on their walks in Ashdown Forest. Over the years, the two visited the bridge, dropping sticks upstream and seeing whose came out first under the bridge. For centuries, the bridge was called Posingford Bridge, as it still is known on official ordnance maps. Soon after the books gained in popularity and people realized that it wasn't merely a fictional place in the Hundred Acre Wood, this once unassuming bridge became popularly known as Poohsticks Bridge. It now attracts more than 35,000 visitors per year. (The bridge has various spellings on maps, signs, and pamphlets. As Milne called the game Poohsticks, we as literary purists will refer to it as Poohsticks Bridge.)

Among the most beloved and memorable images from the Hundred Acre Wood is Christopher Robin leaning over a wooden rail of Poohsticks Bridge, Piglet gently touching Pooh's side. Tenderly drawn, it celebrates the simple pleasures of childhood. For little ones, the game is an entertaining delight with the water. For adults, the site is a bridge to our own childhoods. Giving our children the real Poohsticks experience feels like providing them with an important cornerstone of childhood.

You may be curious to know which came first—the *game* or the *story*? Did Christopher Robin first drop a stick in the stream below and did his father, lovingly watching his son's fascinations and games, then write a little story about it? Or was it the other way around? In the story "*In Which* Pooh Invents a New Game and Eeyore Joins In," Pooh originally plays a game he calls "Poohfir-cones." He eventually decides it is easier to mark and identify sticks. The game forever changed in name. Perhaps the real-life game started with fir-cones. Christopher Robin himself says he can't remember and wonders if it really matters. He wrote, "The

Beloved, humble,
and immortal
Poohsticks Bridge

stories became a part of our lives; we lived them, thought of them, spoke them. And so, possibly before, but certainly after that particular story, we used to stand on Poohsticks Bridge throwing sticks into the water and watching them float away out of sight until they re-emerged on the other side."

Poohsticks Bridge may be among the first places you want to visit when you arrive in the forest. If so, you may find your introduction to Milne a hushed and muted one, a bit like him as a person. He would have liked it that way. Signage is slim. Be watchful as you walk from the "Pooh Car Park," one of the few overt indicators you have slipped into the Hundred Acre Wood, to the bridge. In keeping with the quiet and gentle nature of the books, this famous place in children's literature is only subtly noted. Look for small signs with yellow arrows. Etched on leaning wooden posts is "Pooh Bridge."

There will be much excitement in the air, but there is no hurry to get to the bridge. There are surprises along the way, so go slow. Suggest to your little ones that they look closely when they look down. Somewhere along the path you will find a miniature Pooh house. It is a tiny wooden door and a bell ringer—a small shrine to Pooh and his friends. Peeking inside the hollow of the tree, you will find gifts for Pooh and friends, from honey pots to handwritten letters. Written by adults and children, the notes to Winnie-the-Pooh, Piglet, Eeyore, and other animals of the Hundred Acre Wood provide a glimpse into the meaning of the stories and settings for so many people.

Surprises along the footpath to Poohsticks Bridge

Notes to Pooh and His Friends

Composed on sensible lined note paper in adult handwriting:
"To Piglet, Lots of love to you at Easter. Thank you for feeding my inner child. Love, Jeffrey"

In a child's scrawl, accompanied by a hand-drawn portrait of Winnie-the-Pooh:
"To Winnie the Pooh. I have two books that have you in them and I have read them and I am going to read them a gen because they are so good and I've got a film and ear rings and a teddy bear of you and tiger and eyore and pigglet and the boring rabbit. Love Freya (age 9)"

Written on paper hastily torn from mum's diary:
"Dear Winnie the Pooh and Piglet. Hope you have a lovely Easter. Enjoy the scrummy yummy Easter eggs and for Winnie the Pooh, hope you enjoy the scrummy honey Easter eggs. You are epic! Love, Elena."

A rather phonetic note from a young fan with a thick pink felt marker:
"To poo bir - I hop you ar having a nic dy. Love Bethan"

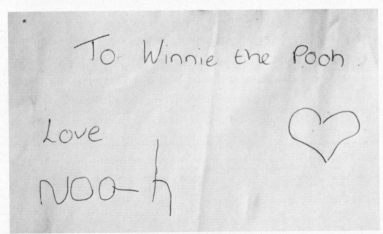

Childhood is a time when imaginary friends feel real.

How do we play Poohsticks and why do we cherish it so?

Requiring only a stick, a stream, and a bridge, it is one of the simplest games in the world, a sport as elemental as it is affable. It is likely even our grandparents and parents played it as children. Even if it is game you have never played, I can assure you that the rules are not so complex that it is too late to learn. Stand upstream on a bridge with a merry band of competitors. Drop your stick—or a pine cone, if so desired—into the river. Hurry to the other side to see whose stick has come out from under the bridge first. It is simple, mildly competitive, and pure Milne. Though athletic and mathe-matical, Milne's game was free of any real strategy and calculation. Even if we think we are strategizing, he seems to joke in the story, our sticks flow with the river current. We may think we can assert our will into the game, but the outcome is at the mercy of forces we do not control. It is a game mainly of chance, reminding us of the fun that can be had in the simple and natural.

There are better times than others to play the game here. Sum-mer weekends are busier, though early summer mornings are not. It also depends on how you like your rivers. The game is swift after winter storms, more languid in summer. On a particularly blustery and windy autumn day, I drove from London to the forest. I nearly turned back as my car was pelted so hard by falling chestnuts and acorns that it sounded like a war zone. If these are the conditions you encounter, you may be inclined to turn back, but don't. Warm blustery days are invigorating if they are not wet. You will then have the bridge to yourself and the stream will be lazy—perfect condi-tions for Poohsticks. Autumn can often be a warm and beautiful time as well, with oaks and maples aflame, dropping glowing leaves like cinders into the stream and on paths scattered with twigs and acorns. By spring, when new green leaves are emerging, the river is sparkly and low again and the woods are electrified with bright car-pets of bluebells.

Whatever time of year you visit, in kindness to the trees and people who live here, do bring your own sticks to lessen the impact of sporty Pooh pilgrims on this special place.

A tributary to the Medway flows under the bridge.

Poohsticks Bridge is located in a medieval-era settlement known as Posingford Farm and is surrounded by Posingford Wood. Local historians believe there have been variations of bridges here as long as people have lived on the farm across the stream, as goods and people needed transport to and from the village of Hartfield and beyond.

In nearly a century since the books popularized the bridge, it has been rebuilt several times, not without controversy and national headline news. What we see now is a splendid blending of fact and fiction—a real place straight from the pages of the Hundred Acre Wood and *The House at Pooh Corner*. When Shepard visited Ashdown Forest for inspiration, he made realistic sketches of the forest. For the bridge, he changed the illustration to suit his own artistic vision. Today the bridge is a wonderful example of life imitating art imitating life, as it is a replica of his original drawings for the Pooh books.

The bridge had fallen into a state of disrepair in the 1940s and there was an idea to rebuild it in a more narrow fashion to save on construction costs. Local people had much to say about the proposed change in the bridge's historical aspect. One of these was a keen horsewoman named Pamela Munn. She lived in Posingford Wood, was very attached to the area, and was a casual meet-on-footpaths acquaintance of the Milnes. She had also read the Winnie-the-Pooh stories to her children and felt the bridge was a treasure. When she learned about the plans to reconstruct Poohsticks Bridge in the narrower manner of a footpath rather than a wider bridle path, she became "possessive about the bridge in a very positive way," her son Charles said. She worked with the local council to assure the bridge would have its historical bridle path width restored, and she demonstrated that she drove her horses across the bridge. Planners were swayed and the bridge you see today owes its width to her.

In 1979, the bridge was reconstructed again with much national fanfare. Imagine for a moment what the characters of the Hundred Acre Wood would be thinking were they in attendance. Paparazzi would have intimidated Pooh. Rabbit would have lined up everyone to be sure their shoes were polished. Tigger would have bounced some cameramen into the river. And Eeyore? Moaning, perhaps a bit dismayed to be at the back of the crowds. The very real and very unassuming Christopher Robin, then a fifty-eight-year-old bookseller living in Dartmouth, Devon, was there. He ceremoniously cut the tape to the new bridge. As television cameramen jostled to capture the scene, he tossed sticks into the stream below, his last game of Poohsticks at the bridge his father immortalized.

After years away from Hartfield, he had also been working to preserve Ashdown Forest from private purchase. Over his lifetime, Poohsticks Bridge had become an important part of English cultural heritage, he felt. Contributions for bridge reconstruction came from Methuen (Milne's original publishers), Pooh fans around the world, the East Sussex County Council, and the National Westminster Bank.

The bridge made news again during another restoration in 1999. It was a complete rebuild. The East Sussex County Council had approached the Walt Disney Corporation, which has certain licensed rights to Winnie-the-Pooh, to provide financial assistance to rebuild the bridge. What followed was local and national resistance to Disney's contribution. As a bridge in England made famous by an English writer and an English illustrator, people wanted it to remain an icon of English heritage and free of any other influences. Fittingly, it was rebuilt by a local builder using locally grown green oak. That is the bridge you see today on your visit.

One of two bridges at the World Poohsticks Championship

World Poohsticks Championship

Every March, when daffodils are at their height, normally buttoned-down adults dust off Pooh and Tigger costumes to play a big game of Poohsticks in Oxfordshire. Voted by *Countryfile* magazine as Britain's "Favourite Quirky Event," the World Poohsticks Competition takes place on bridges between Little Wittenham and Dorchester-on-Thames. Sponsored by the Rotary Club of Oxford Spires, the game is magnificently played by hundreds of people on two bridges—one for individual competitions and another for groups. The official low-key game as we know it is slightly modified. The finish line is farther downstream from the bridge, resulting in cheers as people watch their sticks catch a new current and overtake another stick, or moans when sticks fall behind. A jaunty man wearing a nautical hat and holding a fishing net retrieves sticks.

A father, son, and cuddly friend at the World Poohsticks Competition

The event originated in 1984 following the closure of the Oxford University Poohsticks Society which held an annual competition. The lockkeeper at Day's Lock noticed that people snapped branches from hedges in the area to play the sport over the bridges even though it was hundreds of miles north of Poohsticks Bridge in East Sussex. He decided to put sticks in a collection box with the idea to aid the Royal National Lifeboat Institution (RNLI). It grew to become the event it is today. Proceeds are split between the Rotary's projects and the RNLI. It has been broadcast on foreign television in Russia, Japan, and the Czech Republic and attracts people from diverse countries including the United States, Japan, Kenya, and Australia.

A charm of bygone childhood infuses the event with the atmosphere of a village fete, with face painting, old-fashioned games, and booths selling tea and coffee, cakes and biscuits. In one queue, people stand for sausage and bacon sandwiches. In another, children wait to unleash their inner Tiggers in the bouncy castle. Toddlers amble about the bridges and grass dragging or hugging their stuffed Pooh bears and Eeyores, their eyes shaded by sunhats covered in characters of the Hundred Acre Wood.

Ben Guynan, a father of two, brought his family to the championship. "I always enjoyed the stories as a child and introduced my boys to them. My other half is Russian and they often watch the Russian version of Pooh, which is great fun and slightly different from the original tales." He said one morning over breakfast, the subject of Poohsticks came up. His wife had never heard of it. He researched online and discovered the World Poohsticks Championship. He said, "I turned forty and it's my goal to try forty new

Stellan, Tess, and August Aalto at the World Poohsticks Championship, 2014

challenges this year. I wanted to include a number of quirky, fun and very British events that were family-friendly. We all loved the experience, and plan to return next year—costumed up and competitively-charged." (Full-disclosure: my pink Poohstick beat Ben's yellow Poohstick, though a three-year-old's green Poohstick beat us both.)

Rules for Playing Poohsticks in the Forest

1. Bring your own wooden Poohsticks.

2. All sticks should be the same weight or size. If similar looking, paint yours in jaunty colors.

3. Choose a starter to say, "Ready, steady, go!"

4. Competitors stand side-by-side, facing upstream.

5. Leaning over the bridge, stick out your arm so that the sticks are all at the same height from river surface and bridge.

6. At the sound of "Go!" all competitors let go of their sticks. (Sticks should not be thrown or hurled into the water.)

7. Rush to other side of bridge.

8. The first stick to emerge under the bridge has won.

9. Repeat over and over and over and . . .

How to Find Poohsticks Bridge

FROM THE ASHDOWN FOREST Cen-
tre car park, turn left onto the road.
Drive until you reach The Hatch Inn
and turn right. Go over two small
humped-backed bridges and up Kidd's
Hill, a long, wooded hill. There are a lot
of deer around here, so driving carefully not only allows you a chance to
see them, but it's safer for the deer as
well. Once at the top of the hill, turn
left onto the B2026 and go down the
hill toward the village of Hartfield.
On your left, you will find Gills Lap
car park where a brochure will guide
you on two Pooh walks. Just after the
"Chuck Hatch" village sign, turn left
onto a narrow lane that leads to the
Pooh car park. If this car park is full,
do not park in the lane, as this is dangerous. Go to Wrens Warren car park

on the B2026 and take a lovely walk
down to the bridge. You will see the
well-worn path through the woods
to Poohsticks Bridge via the back
left-hand corner of the Pooh car park.

Walking Distances to Poohsticks Bridge from Car Parks

From Gills Lap car park to Poohsticks
  Bridge and back—approximately
  3.5 miles
From Quarry car park to Poohsticks
  Bridge and back—approximately
  2.75 miles
From Piglets car park to Poohsticks
  Bridge and back—approximately
  2.5 miles
From Wrens Warren car park to Pooh-
  sticks Bridge and back—approxi-
  mately 1.75 miles

Directions to the games

Other Wildlife

There are thirty-four recorded species of butterflies in Ashdown Forest, bringing color and sparkle to the forest like flowers with beautiful wings. One of the most spectacular—the purple emperor—is also among the most elusive and is rarely seen. The more common purple hairstreak is difficult to see due to its habit of flying in the tree canopy where it feeds on honeydew. Fritillaries have declined on the woodland forest floor as coppicing is no longer practiced, resulting in greater shade which inhibits the violets that provide food. Gorse and heathers provide food sources for the plentiful but nationally rare silver-studded blue.

The mix of heathland and woodland pools of water also create homes to a particularly rich fauna of damselflies and dragonflies, notably the black darter, brilliant emerald, and small red damselflies. With red legs and slightly smaller than the common red damselfly, the small red damselfly is drawn to shallow pools, streams, and heathland bogs. Searching out places where yellow bog asphodel grows may lead to sightings of them. Ellison's Pond on the Stonehill Road, the pond at the Forest Centre, and the ponds between Ridge Road and Colemans Hatch are all places where they have been seen.

Silver-studded blue male

Brimstone male

Holly blue female

Red admiral

Small copper

Common heath moths are abundant on heathland and moorland.

Olive-green and fuchsia, the elephant hawk moth gets its name from the caterpillar's trunk-like section behind its head.

A hummingbird hawk moth hovers in front of flowers, sipping nectar with its long proboscis.

Rare red damselfly

Golden-ringed dragonfly

Modernism and the Moors

TWO OF THE TWENTIETH CENTURY'S literary giants lived in Ashdown Forest, just a quarter-mile from The Ridge where Charles Darwin had spent the summer some fifty-three years earlier. For three winters between 1913 and 1916, William Butler Yeats and Ezra Pound rented the six-room Stone Cottage near the village of Colemans Hatch. It was an unheard-of arrangement: two of the greatest poets of the English language in close living quarters for months at a time.

Twenty years younger than Yeats and temperamentally different, Pound acted as Yeats' "secretary"—answering correspondence in the morning, as the elder poet's eyesight was deteriorating, and in the evening reading aloud. The idea of this cohabitation was to be free of the obligations of life in London so that both poets would have time and space to pursue their projects without distractions.

The solitude of Stone Cottage and the stark landscape of Ashdown

Stone Cottage near the village of Colemans Hatch

"It is a most perfect and most lonely place and only an hour and a half from London."
—Yeats on Ashdown Forest

Forest cultivated poetic clarity and sharpened their different visions. Able to work in solitude without interruption, Pound and Yeats both benefited significantly from their time in Ashdown Forest. Pound drafted the first set of cantos, translated Japanese Noh plays, and developed other ideas for poetry. The Noh plays inspired Yeats; his play *At the Hawk's Well* has its origins during this creative period.

Talking over poems and hearing the younger American read aloud helped Yeats move his work toward more concrete diction and away from abstraction, literary critics have noted. In the darker winter months, the two men walked the misty valleys and over the open moors of the forest, gorse flowering under slate skies. After supper, it was a short distance to the local pub, The Hatch, with its low ceilings, narrow corridors, and small windows. There they drank a pint or two of cider.

Several decades later, incarcerated in Italy in 1945, Pound wrote Canto LXXXIII, part of the unfinished 120-section epic, *The Pisan Cantos*, which is considered among the greatest modern poetry of the twentieth century. Pound relied on his memory, drifting back to the time he was Yeats' secretary in Ashdown Forest. He recalls thinking he heard wind in the chimney when it was really the sound of Yeats working "downstairs composing/at Stone Cottage in Sussex by the waste moor."

Friends of Ashdown Forest

Since its inception in 1961, the Society of the Friends of Ashdown Forest has been supporting the conservation of this very special area. In that time, this small local society has given the Board of Conservators £700,000 to help purchase tractors, trucks for rangers, maps, brochures and books, picnic seats and tables, tree planting and other landscape features, notice boards, and radio systems, to name but a few. They also assist in the purchase of land that becomes available within or closely adjacent to the ancient pale and return it to common ownership. The Friends have contributed to the purchase of sixty-nine acres at Chelwood Vachery, which is now being revealed to have a fine woodland and water garden constructed in the early twentieth century, and land at the Isle of Thorns. Reflecting their educational objectives, they have also produced films about the forest—*The Threatened Wildlife* and *A Year in the Life of Ashdown Forest*—which are available for sale and viewing at the Forest Centre and can now also be seen on YouTube.

The Friends also run a varied and interesting program of events which includes talks, meetings and walks to encourage conservation and the peaceful enjoyment of the forest, and publish a twice-yearly magazine, *Ashdown Forest News*. Donations to the Society of the Friends of Ashdown Forest help fulfill their aim of ensuring that everyone can enjoy Ashdown Forest and that, in the future, others will also have this opportunity.

To learn more about Ashdown Forest and to help preserve its rich physical, cultural, and literary history, donations can be made at www.friendsofashdownforest.co.uk. Donations can also be sent to:

Friends of Ashdown Forest
The Ashdown Forest Centre
Wych Cross
Forest Row
EAST SUSSEX
RH18 5JP United Kingdom

A snowy winter in Ashdown Forest

METRIC CONVERSIONS

To convert length:	Multiply by:
Miles to kilometers	1.6
Miles to meters	1609.3
Inches to centimeters	2.54
Feet to centimeters	30.5

To convert area:	Multiply by:
Square inches to square centimeters	6.45
Square feet to square meters	0.093
Acres to hectares	0.4
Square miles to square kilometers	2.6

MILNE BIBLIOGRAPHY

Novels

Lovers in London (1905)

Once on a Time (1917)

Mr. Pim (1921)

The Red House Mystery (1922)

Two People (1931)

Four Days' Wonder (1933)

Chloe Marr (1946)

Nonfiction

Peace With Honour (1934)

It's Too Late Now: The Autobiography of a Writer (1939)

War with Honour (1940)

Year In, Year Out (1952) (illustrated by E. H. Shepard)

Collected *Punch* articles

The Day's Play (1910)

Once A Week (1914)

The Holiday Round (1912)

The Sunny Side (1921)

Those Were the Days (1929)

Collected newspaper articles and book introductions

Introduction to *The Chronicles of Clovis* by Saki (1911)

Not That It Matters (1920)

By Way of Introduction (1929)

Story collections for children

A Gallery of Children (1925)

Winnie-the-Pooh (1926)

The House at Pooh Corner (1928)

Poetry collections for children

When We Were Very Young (1924)

Now We Are Six (1927)

Story collections

The Birthday Party (1948)

A Table Near the Band (1950)

Poetry

For the Luncheon Interval (poems from *Punch*)

When We Were Very Young (1924) (illustrated by E. H. Shepard)

Now We Are Six (1927) (illustrated by E. H. Shepard)

Behind the Lines (1940)

The Norman Church (1948)

Screenplays and Plays

Wurzel-Flummery (1917)

Belinda (1918)

The Boy Comes Home (1918)

Make-Believe (1918) (children's play)

The Camberley Triangle (1919)

Mr. Pim Passes By (1919)

The Red Feathers (1920)

The Bump (1920, Minerva Films, starring Aubrey Smith)

Twice Two (1920, Minerva Films)

Five Pound Reward (1920, Minerva Films)

Bookworms (1920, Minerva Films)

The Dover Road (1921)

The Lucky One (1922)

The Artist: A Duologue (1923)

Give Me Yesterday (1923) (or *Success in the UK*)

Ariadne (1924)

The Man in the Bowler Hat: A Terribly Exciting Affair (1924)

To Have the Honour (1924)

Portrait of a Gentleman in Slippers (1926)

Success (1926)

Miss Marlow at Play (1927)

The Fourth Wall or The Perfect Alibi (1928)

The Ivory Door (1929)

Toad of Toad Hall (1929) (adaptation of *The Wind in the Willows*)

Michael and Mary (1930)

Other People's Lives (1933) (or *They Don't Mean Any Harm*)

Miss Elizabeth Bennet (1936) (based on *Pride and Prejudice*)

Sarah Simple (1937)

Gentleman Unknown (1938)

The General Takes Off His Helmet (1939) in *The Queen's Book of the Red Cross*

The Ugly Duckling (1941)

Before the Flood (1951)

Films

Michael and Mary (1931)

The 1963 film *The King's Breakfast* was based on Milne's poem of the same name.

SOURCES

"Amundsen's South Pole Expedition." Wikipedia. http://en.wikipedia.org/wiki/ Amundsen's_South_Pole_expedition.

Ashdown Forest. "Forest History— Three winters at Stone Cottage," *The Volunteer*, Issue 19 July–Sept. http:// www.ashdownforest.org/management/ volunteers/docs/NEWSLETTER_19.pdf.

Ashdown Forest. "Heathland Conservation." http://www.ashdownforest.org/ management/heathland.php.

Ashdown Forest. "Management Planning for Ashdown Forest Lowland heathland," January 2012. http://www.ashdownforest. org/wild/environment/docs/Heathland_ Feature_mgt_Jan_2012.pdf.

Ashdown Forest. "People on the Forest." http://www.ashdownforest.org/enjoy/ history/people.php

Ashdown Forest. "Special Areas of Conservation." http://www.ashdownforest.org/ governance/statutory/sac.php.

Ashdown Forest. "Statutory Designations." http://www.ashdownforest.org/ governance/statutory.php.

Ashdown Forest. "Wild Flowers and Trees on Ashdown Forest." http://www. ashdownforest.org/wild/docs/List_ Wild_Flowers_Trees.pdf.

Balmoral: Scottish Home to the Royal Family. http://www.balmoralcastle.com/.

BBC Films. "The Real World of Winnie-the-Pooh." *Homeground*. South East Film and Video Archive.

BBC. "Meat-Eating Plants." http://www.bbc. co.uk/nature/life/Drosera#p005fq51.

BBC. "Winnie the Pooh Tops Children's Favourite Book Poll." 2 June 2014. http:// www.bbc.co.uk/news/entertainment-arts-27664081.

BBC Southern Counties Radio. "A Real Display of Flying Skill!" Interview with Tom Mitchell. 29 September 2005. http:// www.bbc.co.uk/history/w2peopleswar/ stories/28/a5958228.shtml.

"Bibliography of Medieval Hunting Treatises." Archives de littérature du Moyen Âge. http://www.arlima.net/ad/ chasse.html.

Botanical Society of America. "Drosera— the Sundews." http://botany.org/ Carnivorous_Plants/Drosera.php.

Brickell, Christopher, ed. *The Royal Horticultural Society Encyclopedia of Plants and Flowers*. London: Dorling Kindersley, 2006.

British Deer Society. "Species." http://www.bds.org.uk/deer_species_overview.html.

British Monarchy. "History." http://www.royal.gov.uk/theroyalresidences/balmoralcastle/history.aspx.

British Trust for Ornithology. "Tracking Cuckoos to Africa . . . and Back Again." http://www.bto.org/science/migration/tracking-studies/cuckoo-tracking.

Buckhurst Estate. http://www.buckhurstpark.co.uk/.

Chandler, Arthur. *E. H. Shepard: The Man Who Drew Pooh*. West Sussex, UK: Jaydem Books, 2000.

Christian, Garth. *Ashdown Forest*. Sussex, UK: Farncombe & Co., 1967.

"Christopher Robin Milne in CNN Ashdown Forest Segment." YouTube video. https://www.youtube.com/watch?v=UB1nXlQgkKU.

Cobb, Edith. "The Ecology of Imagination in Childhood." *Daedalus* 88, no. 3 (1959): 537–548.

Cobbett, William. Sussex journal entry of 8 January 1822, in *Rural Rides*. London, 1982.

Commons Registration Act 1965. The National Archives. http://www.legislation.gov.uk/ukpga/1965/64.

Cottell, R. "Linking Geology and Biodiversity." English Nature Research Reports, no. 562. http://www.cbd.int/doc/pa/tools/Linking%20Geology%20and%20Biodiversity%20(part%201).pdf.

Countrylife. "In an English Garden." 19 May 2005. http://www.countrylife.co.uk/fresh-on-the-market/in-an-english-garden.

Crowborough Life. "Rare Short-Toed Eagle: Bird Watchers Flock to the Ashdown Forest After a Rare Short-Toed Eagle Has Been Spotted There." 17 June 2004. http://crowboroughlife.com/rare-short-toed-eagle-2533/.

Darwin, Charles. *The Correspondence of Charles Darwin: Volume 8: 1860.* Edited by Frederick Burkhardt, Janet Browne, Duncan M. Porter, and Marsha Richmond. Cambridge, UK: Cambridge University Press, 1993.

Darwin, Charles. *Insectivorous Plants.* London: John Murray, 1875. http://darwin-online.org.uk/EditorialIntroductions/Freeman_InsectivorousPlants.html.

Davis, Wade. "George Mallory Died Climbing Everest. His Great War Letters Reveal Why For Him, and Many of His Generation, Life Had to Be Lived to the Full." *The Daily Mail.* 29 November 2012. http://www.dailymail.co.uk/news/

article-2240144/George-Mallory-died-
climbing-Everest-His-Great-War-letters-
reveal-life-lived.html.

Davis, Wade. "Wade Davis on Mallory's
Motivation to Scale Everest." YouTube
video. 9 July 2012. http://www.youtube.
com/watch?v=jOlpoAOydGA.

Duff, David. *Victoria and Albert*. New York:
Taplinger, 1972.

Dean, Lewis. "A. A. Milne Worked as a Spy."
East Grinstead Courier. 8 May 2013.
http://www.eastgrinsteadcourier.co.uk/
Winnie-Pooh-author-AA-Milne-war-spy/
story-18924289-detail/story.html.

Eccelstone, Paul. "Anger over Management
of Ashdown Forest." *The Telegraph*. 25
May 2007. http://www.telegraph.co.uk/
earth/earthnews/3295090/Anger-over-
management-of-Ashdown-Forest.html.

Featherstone, Alan Watson. "Scots pines,
Pinus sylvestris." Trees for Life. http://
www.treesforlife.org.uk/tfl.scpine.html.

Flood, Alison. "Winnie the Pooh Author
A. A. Milne Was First World War
Propagandist." *The Guardian*. 26 April
2013. http://www.theguardian.com/
books/2013/apr/26/milne-first-world-
war-propaganda.

Forest Row Film Society. "50 Years Ago:
Newsreels of President Kennedy in
Forest Row." http://forestrowfilmsociety.

org/news/2013/06/50-years-ago-
newsreels-of-president-kennedy-in-
forest-row/.

Forestry Commission. "About the Horse
Chestnut." http://www.forestry.gov.uk/
website/forestresearch.nsf/ByUnique/
INFD-6KYC7M.

Friends of Ashdown Forest. http://www.
friendsofashdownforest.co.uk/.

Gale, W. K. V. *Ironworking*. Oxford: Shire
Publications, 1981.

Gleave, Josie, and Issy Cole-Hamilton.
"A World without Play: A Literature
Review." Play England. January 2012.
http://www.playengland.org.uk/
media/371031/a-world-without-play-
literature-review-2012.pdf.

Glyn, Philip J., and Hew D. V. Prendergast.
Ashdown Forest: An Illustrated Guide.
Essendon Press, 1995.

Goodman, Ruth. *How to Be a Victorian*.
London: Viking, 2013.

Gray, Peter. "As Children's Freedom Has
Declined, So Has Their Creativity."
Psychology Today. 17 September 2012.
http://www.psychologytoday.com/blog/
freedom-learn/201209/children-s-freedom-
has-declined-so-has-their-creativity.

Hageneder, Fred. "Yew: A History."
The Ancient Yew Group.
http://www.ancient-yew.org/mi.php/
yew:-a-history-by-fred-hageneder/122.

Harris, Paul. "Found . . . The Sketch That
First Captured Magic of Poohsticks:
Original Drawing Depicting Christopher
Robin, Piglet And Pooh Playing Game
Emerges after 85 years." *The Daily Mail.*
20 November 2013. http://www.
dailymail.co.uk/news/article-2510891/E-
H-Shepards-Winnie-Pooh-sketch-
captured-magic-Poohsticks-found.html.

Harrison, Shirley. *The Life and Times of the
Real Winnie-the-Pooh: The Teddy Bear
Who Inspired A. A. Milne.* Barnsley:
Remember When, 2011.

Harveys: The Sussex Brewers. http://www.
harveys.org.uk/.

Heale, Edna. *Wives of Fame: Mary Living-
stone, Jenny Marx and Emma Darwin.*
London: Sidgwick & Jackson, 1986.

Henderson, Bruce. "Who Discovered the
North Pole?" *Smithsonian.* April 2009.
http://www.smithsonianmag.com/
history/who-discovered-the-north-
pole-116633746/?no-ist.

High Weald Area of Outstanding Natural
Beauty. http://www.highweald.org/
learn-about.html.

High Weald Area of Outstanding Natural
Beauty. "High Weald Biodiversity
Statement." http://www.highweald.org/
about-the-high-weald-unit/news/2203-
biodiversity-statement.html.

High Weald Area of Outstanding Natural
Beauty. "High Weald AONB
Management Plan." http://www.
highweald.org/high-weald-aonb-
management-plan.html.

High Weald Area of Outstanding Natural
Beauty. "Statement of Significance."
http://www.highweald.org/high-weald-
aonb-management-plan/statement-of-
significance.html.

Hubbard, Kate. *Serving Victoria: Life in the
Royal Household.* London: Vintage, 2013.

Joint Nature Conservation Committee.
"Special Areas of Conservation." http://
jncc.defra.gov.uk/page-23.

Joint Nature Conservation Committee.
"UK Lowland Heathland Habitat." http://
jncc.defra.gov.uk/page-1432.

Kellert, Stephen. "Building for Life:
Designing and Understanding the
Human–Nature Connection." Children
and Nature Network. http://www.
childrenandnature.org/downloads/
Kellert_BuildingforLife.pdf.

Kim, Young-ha. "Be an Artist, Right Now!" TEDxSeoul Talks. July 2010. http://www. ted.com/talks/young_ha_kim_be_an_ artist_right_now/transcript.

Kirby, Peter. *Forest Camera: A Portrait of Ashdown*. Poundgate, Sussex: Sweethaus Press, 1998.

Klass, Polly. "A Firm Grasp on Comfort." *The New York Times*. 11 March 2013. http://well.blogs.nytimes.com/2013/03/11/ a-firm-grasp-on-comfort/?_php=true&_ type=blogs&_r=0.

Krahnstoever Davison, Kirsten, and Catherine T. Lawson. "Do attributes in the physical environment influence children's physical activity? A review of the literature." International Journal of Behavioral Nutrition and Physical Activity 3, no. 19 (2006). doi:10.1186/1479-5868-3-19. http://www.ijbnpa.org/ content/3/1/19.

Lerer, Seth. "After the Norman Conquest, English and Its Afterlife". In *The Cambridge History of Medieval English Literature*, edited by David Wallace, 7–34. Cambridge: Cambridge University Press, 1999. http:// universitypublishingonline.org/ cambridge/histories/chapter.jsf? bid=CBO9781139053624&cid=CBO978113 9053624A006.

Lewes District Council. "Map Showing the Part of the District within the 7 km of Ashdown Forest." http://www.lewes.gov. uk/Files/plan_7km_Ashdown_Forest_ Zone.pdf

Lichtman, Flora, and Sharon Shattuck. "The Animated Life of A. R. Wallace." *The New York Times* video. 4 November 2013. http://www.nytimes.com/video/ opinion/100000002534565/the-animated-life-of-a-r-wallace.html.

Linnean Society of London. http://www. linnean.org.

"List of Largest United States Forests." Wikipedia. http://en.wikipedia.org/wiki/ List_of_largest_United_States_ National_Forests.

Louv, Richard. *Last Child in the Woods: Saving Our Children From Nature-Deficit Disorder*. Chapel Hill: Algonquin, 2008.

Louv, Richard. "Nature Play Teaser No. 2." YouTube video. https://www.youtube. com/watch?v=A6fipLe8go4.

Longenbach, James. *Stone Cottage: Pound, Yeats, and Modernism*. New York: Oxford University Press, 1988.

Longenbach, James. "The Odd Couple—Pounds and Yeats Together." *The New York Times*. 10 January 1988. http://www. nytimes.com/1988/01/10/books/the-odd-couple-pound-and-yeats-together.html.

Longley, Edna. *Yeats and Modern Poetry.* Cambridge: Cambridge University Press, 2014.

Martin, David, and Barbara Martin. "A Brief Archaeological Interpretive Survey of Cotchford Farm, Hartfield, East Sussex." Archaeology South-West, Institute of Archaeology, University College London, 1997.

Mawer, A., and F. M. Stenton. "Ashdown Forest." *The Place-Names of Sussex.* Vol. VI. Cambridge: Cambridge University Press, 1929.

McDowell, Edwin. "Winnie Ille Pu Nearly XXV Years Later." *The New York Times.* 18 November 1994. http://www.nytimes.com/1984/11/18/books/winnie-ille-pu-nearly-xxv-years-later.html.

Mid Sussex District Council. "Landscape Character Area 6: High Weald." 2005. http://www.midsussex.gov.uk/media/LCA10pt3CA06HighWeald.pdf.

Milne, A. A. "A. A. Milne Speaks (1929)." YouTube video. http://www.youtube.com/watch?v=3Sr3-541IIw.

Milne, A. A. *The House at Pooh Corner.* Wren Library, Trinity College, University of Cambridge. Add. MS. c.200.

Milne, A. A. *It's Too Late Now: The Autobiography of a Writer.* London: Methuen, 1939.

Milne, A. A. Letter from A. A. Milne to E. H. Shepard, dated 18 January 1925, EHS/C/4/1 E. H. Shepard Archive, University of Surrey.

Milne, A. A. Letter from A. A. Milne to E. H. Shepard, undated probably 1925, EHS/C/4/1 E. H. Shepard Archive, University of Surrey.

Milne, A. A. Letter from A. A. Milne to E. H. Shepard, 25 June 1925, EHS/C/4/1 E. H. Shepard Archive, University of Surrey.

Milne, A. A. *Mr. Pim Passes By.* Aeterna, 2010.

Milne, A. A. *Peace with Honour.* London: Methuen, 1934.

Milne, A. A. *Toad of Toad Hall.* London: Methuen, 1981.

Milne, A. A. *Winnie-the-Pooh.* Wren Library, Trinity College, University of Cambridge. Add. MS. c.199.

Milne, A. A. *Winnie-the-Pooh: The Complete Collection of Stories and Poems.* Glasgow: Egmont Books, 1994.

Milne, Christopher. *The Enchanted Places.* London: Penguin, 1974.

Morris, Holly. "The Lure of Everest." *The New York Times Sunday Book Review.* 2 December 2011. http://www.nytimes.com/2011/12/04/books/review/into-the-silence-the-great-war-mallory-and-the-conquest-of-everest-by-wade-davis-book-review.html?pagewanted=all.

Moss, Stephen. "Natural Childhood." National Trust. http://www. nationaltrust.org.uk/ document-1355766991839/.

Mowl, Timothy. *Gentlemen Gardeners: The Men Who Recreated the English Landscape*. Stroud, Gloucestershire: The History Press, 2004.

Musgrave, Toby, Chris Gardner, and Will Musgrave. *The Plant Hunters: Two Hundred Years of Adventure and Discovery around the World*. London: Ward Lock, 1988.

Nabhan, Gary Paul, and Stephen Trimble. *The Geography of Childhood: Why Children Need Wild Places*. Boston: Beacon Press, 1994.

National Wildlife Federation. "Health Benefits." http://www.nwf.org/be-out-there/why-be-out-there/health-benefits.aspx.

Natural England. "European Site Conservation Objectives for Ashdown Forest Special Protection Area Site Code: UK9012181." http://www.naturalengland.org.uk/Images/UK9012181-Ashdown-Forest-SPA_tcm6-32260.pdf.

Natural England. "Guidance for assessing landscapes for designation as National Park or Area of Outstanding Natural Beauty in England." http://www.naturalengland.org.uk.

Nelson, William, ed. *Manwood's Treatise of the Forest Laws*. 4th ed. London: 1717.

New Forest Official Visitor Site. "Pigs in the New Forest (Pannage)." http://www.thenewforest.co.uk/discover/pigs.aspx.

New York Public Library Children's Center at 42nd Street. "The Adventures of the Real Winnie-the-Pooh." http://www.nypl.org/locations/tid/36/node/5557.

New York Times. "A. A. Milne Arrives to See His Plays." 28 October 1931.

New York Times. "Climbing Mount Everest Is Work for Superman." 18 March 1923. http://graphics8.nytimes.com/packages/pdf/arts/mallory1923.pdf.

Parcell, Mike, and Norman Black. "Hartfield Village: An Historical Guide." The Hartfield & District History Group, 2008.

Pembroke College, University of Cambridge Winnie-the-Pooh Society. http://pooh.soc.srcf.net/.

Poetry Foundation. "Ezra Pound 1885-1972, Biography." http://www.poetryfoundation.org/bio/ezra-pound.

Poison Garden. "Taxus baccata, Yew." http://www.thepoisongarden.co.uk/atoz/taxus_baccata.htm.

Pound, Ezra. *ABCs of Reading*. New York: New Directions, 2011.

Pound, Ezra. *The Cantos of Ezra Pound.* New York: New Directions, 1999.

Quest-Ritson, Charles. *The English Garden: A Social History.* London: Penguin, 2003.

Rich, Tim, P. Donovan, P. Harmes, A. Knapp, C. Marrable, M. McFarlane, N. Muggeridge, et al. "Flora of Ashdown Forest." Sussex Botanical Recording Society. September 1996. http://bsbi.org. uk/Flora_of_Ashdown_Forest.pdf.

Rosen, Jonathon. "Alfred Russel Wallace, Charles Darwin's Neglected Double." *The New Yorker.* 12 February 2007. http:// www.newyorker.com/arts/critics/ atlarge/2007/02/12/070212crat_atlarge_ rosen.

Royal Society for the Preservation of Birds. "Red, Amber and Green Explained." 28 May 2009. http://www. rspb.org.uk/wildlife/birdguide/status_ explained.aspx.

Rutter, Clem. "Kent Geology Wealden Dome Simple." http://commons. wikimedia.org/wiki/File:KentGeologyW ealdenDomeSimple.svg#mediaviewer/ File:KentGeologyWealdenDome Simple.svg

Sapsted, David. "Romans Introduced the Rabbit." *The Telegraph.* 14 April 2005. http://www.telegraph.co.uk/news/ uknews/1487787/Romans-introduced- the-rabbit.html.

Satchell, Sam. "Thousands Flock to Ashdown Forest for Rare Glimpse of Short-Toed Eagle." *East Grinstead Courier.* 26 June 2014. http://www. eastgrinsteadcourier.co.uk/Thousands-flock- Ashdown-Forest-rare-glimpse-short/ story-21284062-detail/story. html#ixzz38kg6qWeO.

Shepard, E. H. *Drawn from Memory.* London: Methuen, 1957.

Shepard, E. H. *Drawn from Life.* London: Methuen, 1961.

Shepard, E. H. "A Sketch Made on the Spot When Visited with A. A. Milne." Original Illustrations, Word and Image Department, Drawings Collection, Victoria and Albert Museum, pressmarks I.167. E726-1973.

Shepard, E. H. "Forest study." Original Illustrations, Word and Image Department, Drawings Collection, Victoria and Albert Museum, pressmarks I.167. I169-1973.

Shepard, E. H. "Tree for Wol's House." Original Illustrations, Word and Image Department, Drawings Collection, Victoria and Albert Museum, pressmarks I.167. E725-1973.

Shepard, E. H. "Untitled (Digging a Heffalump Trap)." Original Illustrations, Word and Image Department, Drawings

Collection, Victoria and Albert Museum, pressmarks I.167. E567-1973.

Short, Brian. *The Ashdown Forest Dispute, 1876–1882: Environmental Politics and Custom.* Lewes, East Sussex: Sussex Records Society, 1997.

Sinclair, W. T., J. D. Morman, and R. A. Ennos. (1999). "The Postglacial History of Scots Pine (Pinus Sylvestris L.) in Western Europe: Evidence from Mitochondrial DNA Variation." Molecular Ecology 8: 83–88.

Society of the Friends of Ashdown Forest. "A Year in the Life of Ashdown Forest." One One 2 Media, Natural History Film Archive, 2012.

Society of the Friends of Ashdown Forest. "The Threatened Wildlife of Ashdown Forest." One One 2 Media, Natural History Film Archive, 2012.

Stowe School. "The History of Stowe." http://www.stowe.co.uk/.

Surname Database. "Hartfield." https://www.surnamedb.com/Surname/Hartfield.

Taproot Theatre. "Mr. Pim Passes By." http://taproottheatre.org/mr-pim-passes-by/.

Taylor, Patrick, ed. *The Oxford Companion to the Garden.* Oxford: Oxford University Press, 2006.

Telegraph. "Christopher Robin's Real-Life Happy Ending." 19 October 1998. http://www.telegraph.co.uk/culture/4715991/Christopher-Robins-real-life-happy-ending.html.

Thwaite, Ann. *A. A. Milne: His Life.* London: Faber and Faber, 1990.

Thwaite, Ann. "Obituary: Christopher Milne." *The Independent.* 23 April 1996. http://www.independent.co.uk/news/obituaries/obituary-christopher-milne-1306346.html.

Trinity College, Cambridge. "Great Court Run." http://www.trin.cam.ac.uk/index.php?pageid=378.

Turbervile, George. *The Booke of Hunting.* Clarendon Press, 1576. http://www.archive.org/stream/turbervilesbookooturbgoog#page/n59/mode/2up.

Turner, Tom. *Garden History: Philosophy and Design 2000 BC–2000 AD.* London: Spon Press, 2005.

Village Sign Society. http://www.villagesignsociety.org.uk/.

Watson, George. "The Singular Friendship: Yeats and Pound at Stone Cottage." *The Hudson Review* 42, no. 3 (1989): 421–433.

Wealden District Council. "Ashdown Forest 7 km Special Protection Area." http://www.wealden.gov.uk/Wealden/Planning_and_Building_Control/Planning_Development_Management/Agents_and_Parish_Council_Information/Planning_Agents_Ashdown_Forest_FAQS.aspx.

Wealden District Council. "Ashdown Forest Special Protection Area (SPA), Special Area of Protection (SAP) and Site of Special Scientific Interest (SSSI)." http://www.wealden.gov.uk/Wealden/Residents/Planning_and_Building_Control/Planning_Development_Management/Agents_and_Parish_Council_Information/Planning_Agents_Ashdown_Forest.aspx.

Wealden District Council. "General Guidance on the Habitats Regulations and its impact upon development which requires planning permission within and around the Ashdown Forest." 2014. http://www.wealden.gov.uk/Wealden/Planning_and_Building_Control/Planning_Development_Management/Agents_and_Parish_Council_Information/Planning_Agents_Ashdown_Forest.aspx.

Wealden District Council. "Protecting the Ashdown Forest." http://www.wealden.gov.uk/Wealden/Residents/Planning_and_Building_Control/Planning_Development_Management/Agents_and_Parish_Council_Information/Planning_Agents_Ashdown_Forest.aspx

Wells, H. G., *An Experiment in Autobiography*. Vol. 1. London: Faber and Faber, 1934.

Whitelock, Dorothy, ed. The Anglo-Saxon Chronicle: A Revised Translation. London : Eyre and Spottiswoode, 1961.

Withers, Jane. "Forest Law." Early English Laws. http://www.earlyenglishlaws.ac.uk/reference/essays/forest-law/.

Wickham, Louise. *Gardens in History: A Political Perspective*. Oxford: Windgather Press, 2012.

Wildlife and Countryside Act 1981. http://www.legislation.gov.uk/ukpga/1981/69.

Winnicott, D. W. "Transitional Objects and Transitional Phenomena" in *Collected Papers through Pediatrics to Psych-Analysis*. London: Tavistock Publications, 1958. http://llk.media.mit.edu/courses/readings/Winnicott_ch1.pdf

Wintle, Angela. "Vintage Village Signs: Thousands of Villages Sign Up for a Modern History Lesson." *The Telegraph*. 5 March 2009. http://www.telegraph.co.uk/earth/outdoors/4941964/Vintage-village-signs-Thousands-of-villages-sign-up-for-a-modern-history-lesson.html.

ACKNOWLEDGMENTS

You would think it would be fun and bounce writing this book. Well, yes it was. But there were also unexpected job hazards. Take being pelted by acorns and rock hard horse chestnuts on blustery autumn walks in Ashdown Forest. That hurt. Or walking Gills Lap in a freezing winter storm. My fingers were so blue that I worried the people in the pub where I took refuge: "Oh love, sit by the fire." Or, falling sideways into a prickly gorse bush in summer.

"However," you may say, brightening up, "At least you haven't had an earthquake lately." That is true, no earthquakes. It was not all falling down in heather, bracken, and gorse. There were a few perks along the way. Reading original manuscripts and letters penned by Milne and selecting E. H. Shepard illustrations. Drinking tea at the hearth at Cotchford Farm where Milne shared the first drafts of his writing with his wife and son. Competing in the World Poohsticks Competition.

Most pleasurable has been getting to know Alan Alexander Milne himself. In writing and researching this book, I have grown very fond indeed of the sometimes-misunderstood writer, wishing nothing other than to turn back time and take a walk with him in Ashdown Forest. He was a gentle soul: quiet but observant, rational yet whimsical, independent and stubborn. I have been fortunate to talk with the few remaining people alive who knew Milne, including his gardener George Tasker's son, Peter, who bowled cricket balls to Christopher Robin in the garden and shared his experiences about war with Milne in the garden at Cotchford Farm.

In discovering a new place, a writer soon discovers that, in England, the power of the pub should not be underestimated. They were often my basecamps for writing and researching this book. They include Hartfield's sixteenth-century Haywaggon Inn and the eighteenth-century Dorset Arms down the lane in Withyham. I quickly adopted the mantra "A pint of Harveys, please"—a tribally Sussex ale made with local hops and barley—and the book magically endeared itself to villagers. They were curious about the tall author with the California accent and muddy boots, who worked amidst papers strewn across wooden tables, and burst out of doors for hiking when the sun shone. It is a light-hearted adage that one is considered an outsider in an English village for at least a generation. I'm not so sure about that. This project and I were warmly welcomed by the people I met in Hartfield and Withyham. I was loaned books, told secrets, and taken on many walks. I was shown collections of bird eggs and butterflies, invited to dinners, and welcomed into gardens and village fetes. At the 2014 World Poohsticks Competition in Oxfordshire on Mothering Sunday, I donned a vintage 1920s dress, hat, and gloves to channel Daphne Milne (beating out all other mums for Best Fancy Dress prize). The research, writing, and walking all deepened my understanding of the enduring quality of Milne's stories.

There is much gratitude to express. For research assistance: Sandy Paul of the Wren Library at Trinity College, Cambridge; Sharon Maxwell and Olwen Cotten of the E. H. Shepard Archives at the University of Surrey; Louise Lareau of the Children's Center of 42nd Avenue at the New York Public Library; Elaine Charwat at the Linnean Society, London; Annemarie Bilclough of the Word and Image Department, Drawings Collection, Victoria and Albert Museum, London; Richard Watson, University of Texas, Austin; Christopher Whittick and Elizabeth Hughes of the East Sussex Records Office; and Rosemary Clarkson of Darwin Correspondence Project at Cambridge University. The project would not have been possible without approval from the Estates of A. A. Milne and E. H. Shepard. Thanks to the team at Curtis Brown, Egmont, UK, and Penguin USA for work on text and illustration permissions. Thank you Dr. Hew Prendergast, former director of the Conservators of Ashdown Forest, for expertise in the botanical, cultural, and natural history of Ashdown Forest. Thanks to Pat Buesnel, director of the Conservators of Ashdown Forest; Pat Arnold, chair, the Society of the Friends of Ashdown Forest; and Ashdown Forest Rangers, especially Mike Yates, who gave me a lesser-known tour of the forest. To Nicola Cowee for superb historical sleuthing and behind-the-scenes admin. To the Earl and Countess De La Warr for historical insights and access to Buckhurst and the Five Hundred Acre Wood. Thank you to Alastair and Harriet Johns for opening the doors to Cotchford Farm. Thanks to Mike Parcell of the Hartfield Historical Society for knowledge of local history as well as Amy Parcell's assistance. To authors Bruce Henderson for insights about Arctic and Antarctic explorers, the "astronauts of yesteryear"; Shirley Harrison for initial research assistance; and Paul Matthews for authors connected to Ashdown Forest. To Peter Tasker for insights into A. A. Milne's character and his father's work as gardener at Cotchford Farm. Thanks to many Hartfield and Withyham villagers including Robert and Fenella Murray-Willis, Mike Whitehead of the Haywaggon Inn, James Thompson of The Anchor Inn, Anne Higgins, Charlie Munn, Peter Kirby, Tom Mitchell, Mary Hattel, Nancy Lawrence for hollyhocks, and Dennis and Joan Mercer for sweet peas. Thanks to the Hartfield and Withyham Cricket Clubs. Thank you Mark Weaver, estate manager of Buckhurst. To Mike Harvey with the Chichester Priory Rotary Club. For information about W. B. Yeats and Ezra Pound at Stone Cottage, thanks to Professor James Longenbach and Rosemary Hammond. To tree experts Tony Kirkham at Kew Gardens, Peter Thurman, and Bartlett Tree Experts, as well as Erin Langley, for sharing your expertise and affinity for trees. For photographs of A. A. Milne and his family at Cotchford Farm, thanks to writer Brian Sibley and Tim Jones at Egmont. To Matt Pitts, Woodland and Cultural Landscape Officer of the High Weald Area of Outstanding Natural Beauty. Thank you to the Hart poetry group in Hartfield for contemplation and humor. Thank you Anne Biklé and Patty Lauritzen for reading the manuscript, to fellow Timber Press author Marta McDowell for encouragement. To storyteller and poet Vanessa Underwood who explained her love of reciting Milne stories, and fellow World Poohsticks Championship competitor Ben Guynan. Thanks to Edmund Croft of The Pembroke College Winnie-the-Pooh Society at the University of Cambridge. To Cote Brasserie in Exeter, especially Star (for bubbly word count rewards). To the dozen couples at table forty: your recitations of Milne were inspiring. To the Magdalen Chapter in Exeter, thank you for the perfect writing environment; To Chris Thompson at Philter in Kennett Square, PA, for your support and enthusiasm. To London taxi drivers who tolerated me leaping up, "Here! No, wait, there. Now please back up" while I was sleuthing and photographing. To everyone at Timber Press, especially the wonderful Juree Sondker and masterful Eve Goodman. Thanks to Sheila Ashdown for fine editing and improving the manuscript. To my garden clients, thank you for your understanding when I was under writing deadlines. To my family and friends, near and far, thank you for your warm support. To my friends and gardenistas in the digital landscapes of Twitter and Facebook, your cheerleading has been invaluable. And special thanks to Rolf, August, Tess, and Stellan Aalto for your support and love while I was exploring the Hundred Acre Wood and Ashdown Forest. You are sweeter than honey.

PERMISSIONS AND CREDITS

Illustrations by E. H. Shepard from *Winnie-the-Pooh* and *The House at Pooh Corner*, a preparatory illustration for *Winnie-the-Pooh* by E. H. Shepard held by the Victoria and Albert Museum, sketch including Spanish conquistadores by E. H. Shepard held by the University of Surrey archives, and quotations from letters of E. H. Shepard copyright © The Shepard Trust, reproduced with permission of Curtis Brown Group, Ltd

Quotations from *Winnie-the-Pooh* and *The House at Pooh Corner* by A. A. Milne copyright © The Trustees of the Pooh Properties, reproduced with permission of Curtis Brown Group Ltd, London

Quotations from *Winnie-the-Pooh* by A. A. Milne. Text copyright © The Trustees of the Pooh Properties 1926. Published by Egmont UK Ltd London and used with permission.

Quotations from *The House at Pooh Corner* by A. A. Milne. Text copyright © The Trustees of the Pooh Properties 1928. Published by Egmont UK Ltd London and used with permission.

Images of the Milne family, E. H. Shepard illustrations, and "Methuen's New Books" advertisement provided by Egmont UK Ltd

The letter from Milne to his mother (1886) by permission of Harry Ransom Center at the University of Texas at Austin

Permission to photograph Alfred Russel Wallace's book from The Linnean Society, London

Photographs of Christopher Robin Milne, E. H. Shepard, and H. G. Wells by permission of the National Portrait Gallery

Image of original stuffed animals (1925) by permission of the New York Public Library, Astor, Lenox and Tilden Foundations

100 Acre Wood map and text quoted from *Winnie-the-Pooh* by A. A. Milne, illustrated by E. H. Shepard, copyright 1926 by E. P. Dutton, renewed © 1954 by A. A. Milne, used by permission of Dutton Children's Books, a division of Penguin Group (USA) LLC

Text quoted from *The House at Pooh Corner* by A. A. Milne, copyright 1928 E. P. Dutton, renewed © 1956 by A. A. Milne, used by permission of Dutton Children's Books, a division of Penguin Group (USA) LLC

Photograph of *Winnie-the-Pooh* manuscript by permission of the Wren Library at Trinity College, Cambridge

Other photographs and illustrations

© estate of Marcus Adams / Camera Press, page 19

Ashdown Forest Centre, postcards of village scenes and Ashdown Forest, pages 73, 205, 206 top, 244

Attributed to James Craig Annan, © National Portrait Gallery, page 27

Vivienne Blakey / High Weald AONB Partnership, pages 170 left, 210

David John Brooker, pages 229 bottom left, 230 top left, 276

David John Brooker, Mapping Ideas, including Ordnance Survey data © Crown copyright and database right 2014, page 197 bottom

Nigel Carpenter, courtesy of Royal Ashdown Forest Gold Course, page 215

Richard Carter, pages 270 bottom left and right, 271 bottom

Mark Colvin, pages 270 top, 271 top

Howard Costner, © National Portrait Gallery, London, page 56

Mick Davis, pages 249; 253 top left, top right, middle left, bottom right; 273 top

Matthew Eade, pages 203; 252 top; 253 middle right, bottom left; 254; 273 bottom

Peter Eeles, page 269

Peter Greenhalf / High Weald AONB Partnership, page 217

Michael Harris, page 84

Peter Harrington, page 45

High Weald AONB Partnership, pages 211, 216

Ian Kimber, page 272

Tony Kirkham / RBG Kew, page 96

Courtesy of the Library of Congress, page 19

Vince Massimo, page 37

Graham Nichols, page 253

Nilfanion / used under a Creative Commons Attribution–Share Alike 3.0 license, page 171

Njfoto/Dreamstime.com, page 204

John Palmer and George Slater, page 242

Hew Prendergast, page 197 top

Courtesy of Brian Sibley, pages 44, 48, 49, 97

John Stanton, page 249

Harold Waters, page 185

All other photographs are by the author.

INDEX

A

Aalto, August, Stellan, and Tess, 266

A. A. Milne: His Life (Thwaite), 14

Albert, Prince, 248

Amundsen, Roald, 140

Anchor Inn, Hartfield, 76, 77

animal homes, 96–97

    See also names of individual animal characters

Anne (friend of Christopher Robin), 91, 98–99

AONB (Area of Outstanding Natural Beauty), 75, 210–211

Ashdown Forest, East Sussex

biodiversity in, 210

Board of Conservators, 208–209, 222

buffer zone, 210

composition of, 232–233

ecological habitats in, 218–220

EU designations for, 209–210

films about, 277

flora of, 218–222

geology of, 212

in High Weald AONB, 75, 210–211

iron production in, 215

location, 74

management practices, 222

map, 197

origins of name, 202–203

planted tree clumps of historical significance, 166–167, 185–187, 190–192, 241–242, 243–244

rangers, 128, 162–163

regeneration and protection of, 208

in snowy winter, 276–277

Society of the Friends of, 277

visiting, 198–200

See also names of specific places within Ashdown Forest

Ashdown Forest Centre, 200, 235

At the Hawk's Well (Yeats), 275

B

Baker family, 155

Balmoral Castle, 248

beech trees (*Fagus sylvatica*), 162–163, 234, 238–239

Bee Tree, The, 127–131

Berrow (landscape architect), 86

bilberry (*Vaccinium myrtillus*), 228

biodiversity, in Ashdown Forest, 210

birch trees (*Betula pendula*), 236

bird eggs, 34

birding, tips to enhance the experience of, 250–254

birds, in Ashdown Forest, 249–254

bluebells (*Hyacinthoides non-scripta*), 77, 216, 237

boarding school, 37

Board of Conservators, Ashdown Forest, 208–209

bog asphodel (*Narthecium ossifragum*), 229

M